The Six Pillars of Biblical Power:
Real Theology for the Grass Roots

◆ ◆ ◆

John C. Rankin

TEI Publishing House
West Simsbury, Connecticut
www.johnrankin.org; www.teinet.net

Cover design by Stuart J. Rankin and David R. Clarkin.

First Printing, September, 2008.
Second Printing, July, 2009.
Third Printing, and edit, February, 2011
Fourth Printing, and edit, August 2012.

Content

Introduction

Two Choices

"There are two choices in life: Give and it will be given, or take before you are taken."

I spoke these words spontaneously, in the context of marriage, while addressing an audience of some 550 people at Smith College in Northampton, Massachusetts. It was November of 1994, during one of my series of Mars Hill Forums. My guest was Patricia Ireland, then President of the National Organization for Women (NOW).

I know of nothing in the depths of human experience that is not fully interpreted by this reality. And it is above all a question of power.

What is power? It is the ability to accomplish a desired outcome. The power to give will do that for any healthy goal. But the power to take before you are taken will only devolve into self-destruction. It is ultimately impotent, and equals the inability to attain any desired outcome.

Biblical Theology

The foundational reality of the power to give is the starting point of biblical theology, and for the six pillars of biblical power. And these pillars sum up the whole Bible.

For many people, the word "theology" is mystical, theoretical or terrifying. It all depends on our various experiences with it. The principal fear can be with people or churches that are, in reality or perception, seeking to "shove religion down our throats." I agree – I do not want anything shoved down my throat, especially sideways.

But also for me, true theology it is both energizing and the source for real freedom. "Theology" comes from two Greek roots, *theos* for God, and *logos* for word. It is simply means "God's Word" or "the study of God's Word."

Do we have interest in theology, and its practical effect on our daily lives? Does biblical theology serve human freedom? I argue that biblical theology is the only source for true freedom. Do we pursue qualities such as peace, order, stability and hope; to live, to love, to laugh and to learn? I believe these qualities of the image of God are universal, we all pursue them, and they can only be rooted, fully, in biblical theology.

This is real theology for the grass roots level where all of us live our daily lives, and which, if it percolates from there, can transform nations. I love the study of biblical theology, in depth. And for that reason, I desire especially for its beauty to be grasped by the widest range of people – all of us who want a solid grounding in life. This modest book is thus a simple, yet substantial, summation of real theology, and with the most practical of implications.

Only Genesis

To set the table for the six pillars of biblical power, we need to start with Biblical Theology 101. Namely, what is the nature of the Bible on its own terms? We need to be freed from post-biblical prisms by which most of us see the Bible, whether in terms of church history or various doctrinal grids. There are five basic elements here, and it is the fifth that will define the content of this book.

Story

First, the Bible is the greatest story ever told, indeed, the only fully true story. It is the historical narration of the acts of the Creator on behalf of man and woman, we who are made in God's image.

In other words, it is the story of God's relationship and conversation with us, and ours with one another. Only when we enter into and understand the storyline of the Bible, of these relationships, does true doctrine emerge. Biblical doctrine, or teaching, is rooted in the storyline. It is sterile otherwise.

Creation, Sin and Redemption

Second, we can note that the entire Bible is based on Genesis 1-3 and its three all-defining doctrines of:

Creation → sin → redemption.

The word "fall" can be inserted in place of "sin," as it describes what the first sin did to man and woman – they fell from God's original place, and need to be lifted back. But too, the word "sin" describes both the original fall and its consequences, so I use it as the primary term. "Sin" is a word that is easily misunderstood. It essentially means brokenness of trust, and we all know that from one or many angles.

There are two metaphors we can use to describe these doctrines. The first is directional in nature:

The order of creation → the reversal → the reversal of the reversal.

The second is organic in nature:

The wholeness of creation → the brokenness of sin → the restoration to wholeness.

The order of creation is the root of all truth and reality in time and space:

From the beginning, God established the order of creation, and our lives, according to a set plan that was intended for our greatest joy as his image-bearers. But through a disobedient act of the will, Adam and Eve and the whole human race have submitted to a reversal of that order, and we reap the painful consequences. Sin can thus be understood as a reversal, as brokenness. It is a reversal in that it goes in the wrong direction. It is brokenness in that it breaks relationship with God, with one another and the wholeness of his creation. Following the inception of human sin, God instituted the reversal of the reversal, the redemptive process designed to purchase us back from the slavery of sin, and to restore to us the original purposes, trajectory and wholeness of the order of creation.

The word "redemption" means to buy back out of slavery. Slavery, by definition, is the loss of an original freedom. Thus, we can also define the doctrines of creation, sin and redemption this way:

Freedom → slavery → return to freedom.

In the Apostles Creed and Nicene Creed, this reality of creation, sin and redemption provides the structure of classic Christian confession – God the Creator, Jesus who rescues us from sin as the Redeemer, and the Holy Spirit who sanctifies the redeemed believer.

We cannot participate in the reversal of the reversal without first knowing what the reversal is, and we cannot know what the reversal is apart from first knowing the order of creation. Indeed, I am convinced that the more time we invest into understanding the genius, simplicity and depth of God's order of creation in Genesis 1-2, the more we will have power to understand the rest of Scripture, history and life. We can make a generalization that will repeatedly evidence itself in specific contexts:

Creation is simple and true;

Sin makes things needlessly complex in its dishonesty; and

Redemption restores us to simplicity and honesty.

Occam's Razor (from William of Ockham in the 14th century) is applicable:

Reduce needless redundancies, or the simplest explanation is

usually the truest one.

To put it another way:

Honesty can uniquely afford to keep things simple.

The challenge is to learn the simplicity of the order of creation, and in the midst of the complexity of the reversal, to apply the simplicity, and so arrive at the integrity of the reversal of the reversal. If this rootedness in creation is not secure, then the storms and currents of sin's complexities can drown us, even as we struggle for redemption.

Another way to consider the reality of creation, sin and redemption is by analogy to music. Music requires mathematical and poetic order, and Genesis 1-2 evidences this beautifully. No cacophony as with pagan origin stories. But more profound yet, classical music that ministers to the human soul is rooted in:

Equilibrium → tension → resolution; or

Home → away from home → home again.

Anyone trained in music knows this well. The elements of tension can be repeated, heightened and lengthened in a musical score, and so heighten the glory of the resolution, the return home. Pagan music that stays inside the tension motif reflects its theological error. Wolfgang Mozart (1756-91) was once reputed to run downstairs when awakened by someone playing the piano, and who stopped at a point of unresolved tension. Mozart hit the resolution note and returned to bed, now able to sleep.

God, Life, Choice and Sex

Third, in the order of creation there are four all-defining subjects addressed, with God being the first subject from which all else follows:

God → life → choice → sex.

These are the only four subjects in the universe we ever need to deal with, and they are defined in the order of creation. Or to put it another way, every issue we confront finds its basis in how these four subjects are defined and how they relate to each other.

These subjects equal the content of Genesis 1-2:

> God is sovereign, and his purpose in creation is to give the gift of life, especially human life – man and woman as made in his image to rule over his handiwork. Then comes the gift of moral and aesthetic choice that serves the prior gift of human life. Finally, in the order of creation, is the gift of sex within marriage: here is the power to pass on the gifts of life, choice and sex through procreation to our offspring, to celebrate the height of what it means to be made in God's image.

Or to put it another way, true sexuality is an expression of godly choice that serves the gift of human life that comes from God.

The reversal of the order of creation is thus:

Sex → choice → life →/God.

This reversal order is where promiscuous sexuality employs choice to hide from undesired consequences, and some of these choices injure or destroy human life, all in an affront against God the Creator.

The word "promiscuous" refers to an indiscriminate mixture, and often in terms of multiple sexual partners; but I am using it at its basic level where any sexual mixture outside of marriage is indiscriminate, uncommitted, uncovenantal, and thus promiscuous – from the Latin roots of *pro* +

10

misc[ere], to be "pro-mixture." As well, when I use the word "marriage" in true context, I am referring to that which is heterosexual, faithful and monogamous.

The observation of these terms, as a summation of the content of Genesis 1-2, is an example of real theology at the grass roots.

When we consider the nature of human abortion, with all its pain and betrayals that lead to such desperation for abandoned women, we are dealing head-on with the real world. In the mid-1980s I was addressing a fund-raising banquet for a Crisis Pregnancy Center in Ithaca, New York. In the middle of my talk, I observed how the politics of this debate are framed by the self-chosen labels of "pro-life" and "pro-choice." But I also saw this as a false conflict – both life and choice are good gifts of God, located in the order of creation. We cannot make any choice unless we are first alive, and a choice to destroy the life of another is not an informed choice. In other words, life defines choice.

And, as I thought it out further, I noted that "pro-life" people are overwhelmingly rooted in a biblical sense of the nature of God, and that "pro-choice" people are overwhelmingly rooted in a sense of approving, or at least not disapproving, of sex outside of marriage. Thus the conflict can be portrayed this way:

$$\text{God} \rightarrow \text{life} \rightarrow \;|\leftarrow \text{choice} \leftarrow \text{sex.}$$

And this is really a conflict between the biblical and pagan views of the four subjects of the biblical order of creation:

$$\text{God} \rightarrow \text{life} \rightarrow \text{choice} \rightarrow \text{sex, on the one hand, versus}$$

$$\text{Sex} \rightarrow \text{choice} \rightarrow \text{life} \rightarrow/\text{God, on the other.}$$

In fact, it also proves that there is no debated issue in human history that does not come down to these terms, and how they are defined.

In a debate at Ithaca College sometime later, the topic focused on human abortion. During the question and answer period, I spontaneously said that

11

there were four all-defining subjects in the universe, and introduced in Genesis 1-2. I noticed immediate skepticism from the audience, and in particular there was one student who glared at me, as if to say, "You can't fool me. I know there are far more than four subjects." But as I defined these subjects and applied them to the subject at hand, the skepticism waned noticeably.

Which is to say: I would have likely never made this observation about God, life, choice and sex had I not been engaged with real issues, painful and divisive issues, in the face of genuine skeptics. In these pages, as I focus on the six pillars of biblical power, the backdrop of such prior biblical definitions will always be percolating beneath the surface. They are inescapable.

The Ten Positive Assumptions of Only Genesis

Fourth, in the biblical order of creation, there are ten positive assumptions. When I use the compound term "only Genesis," it is another way of speaking about the content of Genesis 1-2, the order of creation:

1. Only Genesis has a positive view of God's nature (the power to give).
2. Only Genesis has a positive view of communication (the power to live in the light).
3. Only Genesis has a positive view of human nature.
4. Only Genesis has a positive view of human freedom (the power of informed choice).
5. Only Genesis has a positive view of hard questions (the power to love hard questions).
6. Only Genesis has a positive view of human sexuality.

7. Only Genesis has a positive view of science and the scientific method.

8. Only Genesis has a positive view of verifiable history.

9. Only Genesis has a positive view of covenantal law.

10. Only Genesis has a positive view of unalienable rights.

These ten assumptions equal the organization of thought in my first book, *Only Genesis* (now Part I of a larger volume, *First the Gospel, Then Politics* ..., scheduled for 2011). It sets the deeper background to the location and nature of the six pillars of biblical power.

These ten positive assumptions reflect the integrity of biblical content introduced in the order of creation, and define virtually every known subject in the universe, and as infused by the prior definitions of God, life, choice and sex. These ten assumptions also equal the basis for a fully genuine and rigorous liberal arts education.

The Six Pillars of Biblical Power

Thus, fifth, the six pillars of biblical power are distilled from the ten positive assumptions. Both the ten positive assumptions and the six pillars of biblical power are unique, and in their essence and wholeness, they are not found in any pagan origin text or secular construct. These assumptions and pillars are at the core of all that is good in human civilization.

These pillars are ethical in nature. "Ethics" comes from the Greek terms *ethos* and *ethikos*, for "social customs or habits," for how we treat people. And depending on context, "ethics" can be used either as a singular or plural term. "Ethics" as a term, apart from context, is by definition neutral – there are good ethics and there are evil ethics.

The six pillars equal the basis for the most Spirit-filled doctrine possible, doctrine that leads to transformed lives and a transformable world. In fact, these pillars, as believed and lived, lead to the highest standards and accountability to the work of the Holy Spirit in sanctification.

The first four pillars are distilled from the ten positive assumptions, and were placed in parentheses in the listing of the ten assumptions above. The last two pillars are drawn from the order of redemption, which is to say, as a remedy for the broken trust of sin that assaulted the goodness of the first four pillars. Thus, the six pillars are these, and they literally sum up the whole Bible. Jesus repeatedly said that the whole Law is summed up in loving God with all our heart, soul, mind and strength, and thus, in loving our neighbors as ourselves. And as the rabbis have said across the millennia, all else is commentary. The six pillars are my commentary, distilled through my studies and experiences of sharing the Gospel in the face of hostile skepticism:

1. The power to give.
2. The power to live in the light.
3. The power of informed choice.
4. The power to love hard questions.
5. The power to love enemies.
6. The power to forgive.

The Gospel

With these five basic elements of Biblical Theology 101 in place, there are four other crucial terms to be defined, as subcategories of the above.

First is the term "Gospel." It is rooted in the Old Testament Hebrew root *b'sar*, meaning "good news," and is introduced in the assumptions of Genesis 1 when God pronounced his creation "good" (*tov*). Then we see it in the New Testament Greek term *euangelion*, which means "good news," and from which we derive the English term "evangelical." Thus, *tov* and *b'sar* are the language of the order of creation, and *euangelion* is the language of the order of redemption. It is good news that God made the good creation for man and woman as his image-bearers. And it is good news, that in the face of sin, God has provided for our redemption from it. The order of creation is good news, the reversal is bad news, and the reversal of the reversal is good news.

Only Genesis is good news, as God pronounced all he made good. It is the root of the New Testament Gospel where Jesus is the "Messiah," from the Hebrew for "the Anointed One," for Jews and Gentiles alike. The redemptive centrality is clear in the opening words of Mark's gospel: "The beginning of the gospel of Jesus Christ, the Son of God" (1:1). We who claim to be evangelical are those who believe in, live and preach the good news of Jesus the "Christ," from the Greek for "the Anointed One," which fulfills the Gospel of only Genesis. The ten positive assumptions and the six pillars of biblical power are good news.

The Wesleyan Quadrilateral

Second, a vital faith begins with *prima scriptura*, or "Scripture first," that is, the Bible on its own terms. Another way of looking at this is by considering what is historically known as the Wesleyan "quadrilateral" basis for authority in the Christian life:

Scripture → tradition → reason → experience.

This means Scripture – the 66 canonical books of the Bible – is regarded as the inspired and sufficient written word of God. On this basis, we affirm and support all church traditions that are consistent with Scripture, and we set aside those that are inconsistent. Thereafter, reason and intellectual rigor are received as God's gifts and as intrinsic to a biblical worldview to begin with. Finally, the purpose of biblical faith is to experience God's love. With

Scripture, tradition and reason in place, such experience is properly rooted, and it flourishes.

The reversal of the Wesleyan quadrilateral is:

Experience → reason → tradition → Scripture.

This is idolatry, and idolatry can be as explicit as goddess worship or pantheism, or as subtle as a wrong order of priorities. The most perversely successful idolatries worship something "good" instead of the God who made it good. Experience is good, but it is not God. Reason is good, but if untethered from the God who made the mind, it turns ultimately to evil. Tradition is good, but if it supplants Scripture, it becomes an idol. Politics is meant to serve the human good, but it is not God. Even the Bible can be reduced to an idol. We worship God who inspired the Bible, not the book itself. The Bible is meant to lead us to this true worship.

A Radical Faith

Third, biblical faith is radical.

"Radical" comes from the Greek word *radix* and the Latin word *radicalis*, that which is "root level" or foundational. "Radical" is a good word when used properly.

Biblical believers are thus called to be radical, to have a sure foundation that provides balance and strength, quite the opposite of being extreme or fanatical.

To be radical is to be biblical. To be biblical is to be rooted in only Genesis, the only truly radical foundation in history. Thus, the ten positive assumptions and the six pillars of biblical power are radical – the most deeply rooted and foundational realities of how we relate to God and one another.

Radical ethics will lead us to:

16

1. Give when taken;
2. Bless when cursed; and
3. Love when hated.

Or, in other words, we have two choices in life – give and it will be given, or take and it will be taken.

Biblical believers are called to reverse the reversal. The roots of time and history are in Genesis 1-3, so if we wish to be genuinely radical in rectifying the political evils of our time, the order of creation is where we start.

The Image of God

And fourth, from the outset, we are all created in the image of God; we are the crown of his creation. In grasping this reality, we come to understand a common ground that is truly universal.

At a debate in April 1989, at Brown University in Providence, Rhode Island, I spontaneously articulated some elements of the image of God. I was questioned about the issue of rape and incest. A young woman believed that the right to have an abortion should be available to those who became pregnant by such a violent act.

I began to frame my response by looking directly at her and saying: "In your life, are you like me, seeking the qualities of peace, order, stability and hope?" As I spoke these words, I had her eyeball-to-eyeball attention, and the hundreds of students and faculty in the Sayles auditorium came to a hush. The century old seats, bolted to the floor, always creaking at the slightest movement, also ceased their chatter, producing a moment of intense focus. She said, "Yes."

I then said, "Is it also fair for me to assume, that like me, you also seek to live, to love, to laugh and to learn?" Again, the same focus of intensity defined the audience, the seats unmoving, and again she said, "Yes."

So I continued, "Then there is far more that unites us than divides us – we are seeking the same qualities. The question is, in the face of the hell of rape and incest: Does abortion unrape the woman and restore to her the lost qualities of peace, order, stability and hope? Or does the abortion only add further brokenness?"

The room continued its quiet, and I could have left the issue there. I knew that the resonation with the image of God, as represented by these qualities, was so complete in that moment that most students and faculty could answer the question themselves and deduce from there the reality I was addressing.

In the content, pain and deep emotions of such a question, there is the need to draw on and, at least implicitly, identify the six pillars of biblical power. A brief review would show how rape, incest and human abortion oppose these six pillars. The true power of love is needed to redress the false power of rape.

When I spontaneously defined these qualities of God's image – peace, order, stability and hope, to live, to love, to laugh and to learn – they were immediately imprinted in my soul. They sum up well the theological realities of the image of God, and they make an easy acronym, the POSH Ls. I have identified and defined the POSH Ls ever since.

In fact, once in a conversation with a medical doctor at a social function, we came to the question of the image of God. As I set the stage to share this story from Brown, she identified herself as "pro-choice." I said that was not an issue for my purpose in sharing the story, and let it slide. My interest was deeper. So when I came to the point of the rhetorical question, "Does abortion unrape the woman?" I was surprised as she interjected with passion, "No!" In other words, far deeper than a political debate, a mutual resonance of the human spirit was touched. This is the nature of the "first the Gospel, then politics…" as I describe it elsewhere. Winning a debate is easy, but so often pyrrhic; winning an honest relationship in the face of a debate over divisive issues is the Gospel. Then the issues can be looked at honestly and mercifully.

In his 1971 song, "Slip Slidin' Away," Paul Simon addresses both social and theological concerns. In one verse he evokes the prospect of a father traveling a great distance to explain to a young son why he hasn't been there for him. But fear and uncertainty creep in, and upon arrival, the father simply kisses the sleeping boy and leaves. Simon's chorus then defines a truly ubiquitous moment: "Slip slidin' away, slip slidin' away, you know the nearer your destination the more you're slip slidin' away."

This is a fine poetic grasp of the theological nature of human sin – we strive for the qualities of the image of God, but it seems too often that the more steps we take forward, we actually make or yield to more backward steps. The six pillars provide the power to overcome obstacles to the reconciliations we seek.

The Goodness of True Skepticism and the Gift of Thinking

So far, we have sought to define some key elements of Biblical Theology 101, and hence the basis for the six pillars of biblical power.

One pillar is the love of hard questions, and it proves integrally related to the prior three rooted in the order of creation. I have introduced real theology at the grass roots in how I first grasped the God $\rightarrow$ life $\rightarrow$ choice $\rightarrow$ sex nature of only Genesis. So too does my whole theological grasp of the six pillars, and all that constitutes Biblical Theology 101, find root in the fruit of an original and experiential skepticism. And from my experience in first seeking and finding God, I came naturally to embrace the Wesleyan quadrilateral in its foundation for genuine experience.

From age seven, I grew up in a church in the Unitarian-Universalist Association (UUA), and there I was taught to be a skeptic of the Bible. My father had moved from a Presbyterian church where he was affronted by judgmentalness, then from a Congregational church where he was dismayed by serious hypocrisy, and wound up in the UUA because the minister was intelligent and faithful to his wife.

My upbringing was healthy, where my father as a physician loved to care for people, loved and respected my mother (who died just after I finished college), loved the five of us children. My early years were not polluted by poverty, fratricide, divorce or one of a number of other toxins that assault children. Thus, I was free to wonder about the universe. When I was reading an early manuscript of this book to my father, then 90 with failing eyesight, and I came to this juncture, he mused with laughter, and said, "You know John, as a young boy you were always thinking." The gift of thinking – so very precious, and something I have always pursued.

As an eight-year old, in the fall of 1961, our Sunday School teacher read the story of Jesus feeding the five thousand men (plus women and children). She said up front, "And of course, we know that miracles cannot occur." I thought to myself, *Why not?* I was skeptical. She continued to explain how what really happened was that Jesus inspired thousands of selfish people to unstuff their tunics, which were full of bread and fish, and share them with each other, all because Jesus inspired one little boy to bring forth his five small barley loaves and two small fish.

I thought she was explaining too much, even though I had yet to learn of the social impossibility of such in first-century Jewish life, where modern individualism was a foreign concept. The people were away from the town spontaneously, it was late, no provisions had been made, and whatever food they had they would naturally share with one another, beginning with the needs of the children.

Then, in the winter of 1962, our teacher turned to the Old Testament, starting with Genesis. She gave a detailed explanation of how Genesis was a primitive myth among primitive people who did not know science or other modern means of knowledge. So I thought, *If it is a myth, why bother?* I was again skeptical.

Skepticism is good if used in pursuit of the truth. The goal is to test everything equally to see what proves true and what does not. That which proves true can be embraced with confidence, along with the freedom for the risk-taking nature of faith that follows. But skepticism employed to avoid the truth does not serve the good, nor true power. Thus, to be skeptical of the Bible is fine; it is a question of why, and to what end. Truth proves itself to the honest skeptic – and the truth of the six pillars of biblical power proves satisfying.

In reading this portion of the manuscript to my father, he again laughed heartedly and in agreement, quoting the Latin for being "skeptical of skepticism."

In my skepticism of skepticism at this early age, I was rooted in a prior amazement at my existence in the face of an awesome universe. I remember wondering where space ended. To find out, I hitched a ride with Flash Gordon (that will date me) and traveled to the end of the universe. And do you know what we found? A brick wall with the words posted on it, "End of Universe." Now it was a little comforting that in the age of Sputnik that the sign was in English and not Russian. But it was also unsatisfying. What was on the other side? And what was on the other side of the next wall?

Then there were the questions about time and number. What happens one minute after time ends, or what is the biggest number? What is the biggest number plus one? And on and on. No one can deny the reality that this known universe, in which we can measure our existence, is bounded by the necessary and helpful concepts of space, time and number. And we all acknowledge that since we can describe the limitations of these measurement devices, there must be something greater. And yet we cannot wrap ourselves around that which is greater, for we are finite and limited. Where does such a trajectory take us?

A Skeptic Finds the Answer

In the face of this trajectory, I was nonetheless a self-conscious agnostic by age 14. An "agnostic" is usually a term for someone who does not know if there is a God (from the Greek roots *a* + *gnosis*, "to be without knowledge"). But it was an open-ended and positive agnosticism, which is to say I was always impressed by the beauty of the universe and amazed by my own existence and self-awareness. I was open to whatever truth proved to be, open to the idea of God. But I did not know one way or the other in the summer of 1967.

I was in Boy Scout camp, and each Sunday we were required to attend chapel service. One Sunday morning, as I was getting dressed, one of my tent mates was resting on his bunk bed. I asked him why he was not getting ready. He answered, "I am an atheist." So I asked him, "What is an atheist?" He said that it meant he did not believe in God, and all I had to do to get out of chapel was to tell the scoutmaster that I was an atheist. I said, "But I don't know." So I went to chapel.

That September, I began ninth grade ("third form") at South Kent School, a small prep boarding school for boys in the Housatonic highlands of western Connecticut. South Kent had a daily chapel schedule rooted in the Episcopal liturgy.

It was required, but I determined not to participate, saying to myself, *I don't believe this stuff.* So I did not sing, recite, pray, genuflect or take communion. But that proved a "dangerous" thing to do. For while other students were participating at one level or another, I ended up occupying my mind reading the words of the liturgy and hymns, as they were recited and sung. I was interested in the possible existence of God.

On November 1, I was standing outside the chapel in the interlude before walking down the hill to dinner. As the air pricked my spine, I felt alive. It was delightfully cold, and in those rural hills the Milky Way was exceptionally clear that evening – like a white paint stroke against a black canvas. I considered its awesome grandeur and beauty, and then I posed to myself this sequence of thought:

If there is a God, then he must have made all this for a purpose, and that purpose must include my existence, and it must include the reason I am asking this question. And if this is true, then I need to get plugged into him.

I wanted to know either way, and I was convinced that if there were a God, then it would be most natural to become rooted in my origins. To be radical before I knew what radical was. But I wanted verification. The "if" clauses were real.

This was a commitment to myself, in the sight of the universe, in the sight of a possible God. It was in fact a prayer to an unknown God.

One or several evenings later, I was the first student into chapel, taking my assigned seating in the small balcony. As I sat down and looked forward in the empty sanctuary, I said under my breath, "Good evening God." Immediately I retorted to myself, "Wait a minute John. You don't even know if there is a God. How can you say 'good evening' to him?"

But also immediately, I became aware of a reality that was prior to and deeper than the intellect, of a truth that held the answer to any and all of my questions. There was a God, I knew deep within me, and I knew that I had just lied to myself by saying I did not know, even though it was only now that I knew I knew. My heart knew before my mind knew, but as part of the whole that my mind was now grasping. I had yet to speak it (see Romans 10:9-10).

In this moment, God's presence ratified the reality of my belief as I simultaneously discerned a Presence literally hovering over me, filling the entire balcony. And, critically, this Presence was hovering and waiting for my response. It was powerful, inviting and embracing. This all happened within a moment's time, and I realized that I did believe. No sooner had I exhaled my agnostic retort, did I then inhale and say, "Yes I do (believe)." As I did, this literal presence of God descended upon and filled my entire being – heart, soul, mind and body.

Now I knew nothing at the time of the divine name and nature of Yahweh's presence and glory, as experienced by the Israelites in the exodus community with the tabernacle, and later in Solomon's temple. Nor did I know anything of the gift of the Holy Spirit. Yet the grace of God came into my life that November evening, as he but gently crossed my path with a touch of his Presence. I asked an intellectual question in view of an awesome universe, and was answered by the Presence of the awesome Creator.

The Six Pillars

With some Biblical Theology 101 in place, and with the trajectory of my love for hard questions as a key prism for my grasp of such theology, let's look at the six pillars of biblical power. They are transformative for all who would embrace them.

♦ ♦ ♦

Chapter One

The Power to Give

The Dilemma

Can something be destroyed that is not first created? This is the dilemma of pagan religion. There are two ways to define the existence of the universe and human life – through creation or destruction.

On the one hand is the biblical Genesis, in which the eternal God is good, creation is good and human life is good. On the other hand, the most influential of ancient pagan origin stories, the Babylonian Genesis, starts with no concept of original or final goodness. It assumes, but does not explain, the existence of finite, petty, jealous and sexually promiscuous gods and goddesses who beat up on each other and beat up on us. It assumed that the heavens and earth were created by one god, but out of an act of destruction.

This is also known as "dualism" – the most ancient non-biblical concept. Creation and destruction are seen as the opposite sides of the same coin; likewise with good and evil. Accordingly, there is no original and greater goodness that will triumph over evil in the end.

But how can Babylonian religion and paganism make any sense? Does not the power to destroy require a prior power to create what is then destroyed? Unless the gods, goddesses and their undefined habitat were first created, where did it all begin? All pagan origin stories cannot resolve this dilemma, and thus they ratify the uniqueness of the biblical Genesis. Secular humanism and atheism, both philosophical and ethical cognates of the older pagan religions, cannot resolve this dilemma either.

Which satisfies the human soul – creation or destruction?

In the Beginning

The first pillar is the power to give. Genesis 1:1-4 reads:

> In the beginning God created the heavens and the earth. Now the
> earth was formless and empty, darkness was over the surface of the
> deep, and the Spirit of God was hovering over the waters.
>
> And God said, "Let there be light," and there was light. God saw
> that the light was good, and he separated the light from the darkness.

All else that follows in Genesis 1 is the ordered creation of the cosmos,
from the most remote to the most immediate and, in terms of life, from the
most simple to the most complex. At the completion, man and woman were
made in God's image, to be his stewards over his good creation.

This is the origin of the power to give – God gives existence and life
where it did not exist beforehand.

The order of creation (Genesis 1-2) has three key components in the
simple majesty of its opening assumptions:

1. *Yahweh Elohim* (the Hebrew for the LORD God) is the eternal and
   good Creator.
2. The creation is ordered and good.
3. Man and woman are the crown of God's good creation and made
   free.

All is good. There is no presence of destruction.

The Hebrew words for "formless and empty" are *tohu w'bohu*, and this
means that the eternal God brought order and existence to what did not
exist beforehand. It was not a creation *ex nihilo*, "out of nothing" as it were.
The text does not say that, for there is nothing outside of God. Rather, from
within God's nature, he spoke into existence that which was not in place
beforehand. Or, as the writer of Hebrews puts it:

By faith, we understand that the universe was made at God's command, so that what is seen was not made out of what is visible (11:3).

For our sake, the visible was made out of the invisible; what we can grasp out of what only God can grasp. God created the universe and all that is in it in order to give man and woman stewardship in ruling over it, for the joy of loving him and one another. A gift given. Indeed, the Hebrew and Greek words for "grace," *hen* and *charis*, both simply mean "gift." God is gracious; his power is the power to give.

Male and Female: The Grand Design

God is the author of the power to give, and he demonstrates it to man and woman as his image-bearers. The image of God involves many aspects and is summed up in imitating God's power to give. This is why we were made male and female – to give to and receive from each other in a God-ordained equality and complementarity.

Genesis 1:26-28 reads:

> Then God said, "Let us make man in our own image, in our likeness, and let them rule over the fish of the sea and the birds of the air, over the livestock, over all the earth, and over all the creatures that move along the ground."
>
> So God created man in his own image,
> in the image of God he created him;
> male and female he created them.
>
> God blessed them and said to them, "Be fruitful and increase in number; fill the earth and subdue it. Rule over the fish of the sea and the birds of the air and over every living creature that moves on the ground."

When God created "man," the Hebrew word is *adam*, from whence Adam derived his name. The word *adam* does not mean "male" (like *ish* or *zakar*), but it is the principal word for "mankind" or "humankind" – specifically including both male and female, and/or in plural reference.

Thus, *adam* is gender inclusive, and its use throughout the Hebrew Bible in the generic sense means that mankind includes both male and female. Adam took on the name of *adam* as a personal name representative of humanity, representative of the unity God designed for male and female as equal image-bearers of God.

Genesis 5:1-2 makes this explicit: "When God created man, he made him in the likeness of God. He created them male and female and blessed them. And when they were created, he called them 'man.' "

He called them *adam*. Thus, the biblical language is poignantly specific from the outset in a) demonstrating the equality of man and woman, that together they equal "man," and b) that the use of the male pronoun when referring to "man" or "mankind" is inclusive of both male and female.

The "He" of God

This leads us to consider the use of the male pronoun, the "he" of Adam, or better yet, the "he" of God. In Genesis 1:27 we see the use of three pronouns in parallel equality at the end of each line:

his own image = him = them.

We also see the defining parallelism of nouns for these pronouns earlier in each line:

man = the image of God = male and female.

These parallelisms were obvious to the Hebrew hearer and reader, and Genesis 5:2 reiterates the same prosaic clarity – that male and female are "man."

God the Father is above male and female, for both male and female are equally derived from his character, and he is at peace with himself in triune community. He is neither male nor female in the human sexual sense, in terms of a singular sexual identity. God applies female metaphors to himself in Scripture at certain points, but God is called "Father" (see the language of Deuteronomy 32:6; and especially of Jesus' use of "Father" for God) and always uses the masculine pronoun, never is called "Mother" and never is described with female pronouns. God is "he" and not "she."

So, whereas the Hebrew Bible is unique in describing men and women as equally sharing the image of God, the description of God is in masculine terms. The masculine "man" is the designated term to include man and woman, as opposed to the feminine "woman" being the designated term. This is due to the simplicity of the power to give, and accordingly, the important question to ask is not why God is called "he," but why Adam is called "he." Or in other words, the "he" of God is not a designation of being male; rather the "he" of Adam is a designation of the power to give as initially received from God.

Human sexuality, at its deepest core, is designed to be the epitome of where the power to give is expressed in human community, and it is designed for the covenant of one man and one woman in marriage. If we make the mistake of looking at God through the prism of broken human sexuality, then we can end up making him a "male." This is what pagan religions do with male gods and female goddesses.

Adam as male derived the nature of his "he" from God, and not the other way around. God the Father employs all his power in the power to give, to bless and benefit us who are made in his image. And within the Trinity, we see the dynamics of this relationship as based on giving and receiving. God the Father, Son and Holy Spirit are consistently giving honor to each other, and receiving it from each other, in their unified nature.

This is why, as we will see, Genesis 2:24 says a man will leave his father and mother, be joined to his wife and the two of them will become one flesh. The two – male and female – became one because of the prior reality of God, in whom the three are one; and because the image of God requires both male and female in order to reflect the nature of the triune God, where unity and diversity exist together in unity, where diversity is in service to unity. This unity and diversity represented in the two becoming one in marriage reflects the unity and diversity within the triune God. True diversity in service to unity is rooted in man and woman in marriage as the purpose for the image of God.

Human nature is necessarily not atomistic (that is, a stand alone unit); rather it is plural in man and woman. Human sexuality is derivative of God's nature, and that nature is the power to give. In order to give, we must have someone to whom to give. And in order to receive, someone must give to us. The act of giving is based on a need to give – namely, as Jesus said, it is more blessed to give than to receive (see Acts 20:35). Unless the act of giving has an object for its giving, it is aborted, along with the goodness of receiving. In this regard, God's nature within himself is to give and receive – this is the nature of love. The apostle John says that God is love, and this is ethically what is being referenced. We love, he tells us, because God first loved us (see 1 John 4:7-12). And God's love is first expressed in the power to give and receive within the triune community, before Adam and Eve were made in his image.

In the biblical creation, God the Father initiated the power to give as he made man and woman to receive such giving, and this reflected the dependent and needful nature of the human soul. Receiving cannot happen without the prior reality of giving; thus God is the Initiator of all giving. The "he" of God is best understood as reflecting this ethical dimension, and not to be seen as restricted to a human limitation of the male pronoun.

Adam took on the designation of "he" because he was the first human to receive from God, and thus empowered to be the first human to pass on the power to give. In the finitude of human nature, in order to catalyze the cycle of giving and receiving, God first demonstrated his giving to the one who would receive it, and that such a one would then naturally give to another. Giving and receiving is the true nature of all relationships as ordained by God; and in the sexual intimacy of marriage, it reaches its zenith, its most beautiful and complete nature.

This is the line of thinking I was briefly sharing with Patricia Ireland at Smith College in 1994. The subject at that moment was the nature of marriage, and she responded quite positively when I addressed the ethics of the power to give. And thus, I made my observation for the first time: "There are two choices in life: Give and it will be given, or take before you are taken."

We see that Adam received the "he" in his maleness because God designed him to also give to his wife. Or to put it another way, whoever was made first was by definition male, when male is understood in terms of the "he" of God's initiation of the power to give in the order of creation, and not in terms of the "he" of male chauvinisms, which did not happen until the reversal.

Male and Female: The Specifics

In Genesis 1:27, we see the "he" language in the context of the grand design of creation, as theological purpose is outlined. In Genesis 2:18-25, we are introduced to the specifics of the creation of Eve:

> The LORD God said, "It is not good for the man to be alone. I will make a helper suitable for him."

Now the LORD God had formed out of the ground all the beasts of the field and all the birds of the air. He brought them to the man to see what he would name them; and whatever the man called each living creature, that was its name. So the man gave names to all the livestock, the birds of the air and all the beasts of the field.

But for Adam no suitable helper was found. So the LORD God caused the man to fall into a deep sleep; and while he was sleeping, he took one of the man's ribs and closed up the place with flesh.

Then the LORD God made a woman from the rib he had taken out of the man, and he brought her to the man.

The man said,

"This is now bone of my bones
and flesh of my flesh;
she shall be called 'woman,'
for she was taken out of man."

For this reason a man will leave his father and mother and be united to his wife, and they will become one flesh.

The man and his wife were both naked, and they felt no shame.

As God completed the stages of the creative progress defined in the days of creation, we see the idea repeated: "And God saw that it was good." Then on the sixth day, when man and woman were created, they were his goal, the crown of creation, and then the text says, "God saw all that he had made, and it was very good."

Thus, when we read in Genesis 2 that God declares something as "not good," we face a powerful disjunctive. How can something be "not good" in the order of creation? The answer is straightforward: Something was not yet complete.

In Genesis 1, we have the grand design of creation where *Elohim* is the Hebrew name used for God as Creator, who in his essence is greater than the concept of number. Then we have a theological statement that man and woman were made in his image.

In Genesis 2, *Yahweh* is the Hebrew name used for the covenant-making God who gives Adam the initial commands and promises of the creation covenant. Yahweh is the name of the Creator who in his essence is greater than the concepts of space and time.

Thus, *Yahweh Elohim* (the "LORD God" in Genesis 2:4) is he who is greater than space, time and number, whose power is unlimited, whose nature is good and whose power is the power to give. In other words, Genesis 2 describes the specifics of how God made man and woman on the sixth day, whereas Genesis 1:26-28 gives the theological statement and purpose as to why he created mankind.

Accordingly, in Genesis 2:18-25, we have the specifics of how and why the woman was made. God had already made Adam out of the dust, breathed the breath of life into him, and gave him the commandment of freedom (which we will examine in chapter 3). The *adam* of Genesis 2:7 is not referring to an androgynous creature, in the sense that *adam* here could be seen as being male and female in one nature and body. We know this because of the subsequent text that treats *adam* as the proper name for the first male, Adam, one in need of his female complement.

Part of Adam's freedom was his authority over the created order as Yahweh's vassal – the "why" of Adam's existence. So there Adam stood – naked, innocent and free in the presence of his Creator. Yet something was missing. Adam needed a "helper suitable for him." The Hebrew term for "helper" is *ezer*, and it has no sense of subordination whatsoever. In fact, whereas it refers to the act of giving assistance, it is more often used to specify the one who gives the help – to the power to give, which equals God's nature, and human nature in God's image. Its most frequent use in the Hebrew Scriptures is in reference to God himself as the divine helper, and here Eve reflected the image of God as she came to help Adam. In the New Testament, the Holy Spirit is also called the "helper." Here, *ezer* is a word for moral and relational equality, based on a mutual power to give and receive.

In other words, Adam by himself did not fully bear the image of God. We already know this by the text in Genesis 1:27, where the language of mankind and its inclusiveness of male and female is descriptive of the image of God. Here in Genesis 2, we see God demonstrating to Adam his need for a helper. Yahweh declared it was not good for the man to be alone, and then it seems that the subject changes. God brought him the various creatures in order for Adam to give them names.

What does the naming of the animals have to do with addressing Adam's loneliness? It has to do with God demonstrating to Adam the power to give, and how first we must receive from God's hand in order to give to others. We give to others out of the same power, where the act of giving is intrinsically satisfying. In other words, we need to give – we need someone to whom to give, otherwise giving is not possible, and receiving is out of the question. The need to give and receive is provided for within the Trinity, and here God walks Adam through the steps of recognizing that as an image-bearer, he, too, was designed to give and receive.

Now that Adam had received, he was equipped to give, and at the same time he was not complete without someone to whom to give, someone who was his equal. He could give back to God, but as a creature, not an equal. He could not give to an animal and receive back with reciprocity, for he was not an animal. He needed a helper so that he could exercise the power to give, so that reciprocity in giving returns to him. His helper could not be his mirror image – another man. He needed an equal who was also a complement, where between the two they completed each other, where they added unique dimensions the other did not possess.

He needed a woman. Adam needed Eve to give to and receive from in order for the image of God to be complete. He was made for communication, to share with an equal, to not be lonely. And giving must be initiated. Giving begets giving; but if taking is the initiative, then taking begets taking. The former is the prescription for peace. The latter is the prescription for war.

In the Garden, God initiated the power to give, and Adam needed to do the same in order to reflect his image as a male, to reflect the "he." Then Eve, as a female, received, and was thus empowered to give and receive as "she." The cycle of giving and receiving was catalyzed, and either party could initiate the act of giving any time henceforth.

The Garden of Eden and all creation were before Adam, and he was given the power to name the creatures – the power to affirm the goodness of God's created order. This naming process was an initial exercise of his status as God's image-bearer. As Yahweh created, now Adam was given the privilege to be procreative in the fullest sense of the term (to procreate is not only to have children; it is to be creative in all contexts with the resources God gives us in creation). God is the Creator, and Adam was now called to be the procreator. But his procreation was limited when his only relationship here was with the animals. Procreation came as the gift of the Creator, the Father of us all.

Adam was alone, the giving of names is creative, and he also discovered first hand the difference between man and animal. He did not smell like them or look like them; he noticed that the animals were in twos and he was in ones; he was lonely and did not want to mate with any of them.

God taught Adam in this exercise that:

1. He was made in God's image;
2. Animals were not;
3. He was not an animal; and

4. His image-bearing status was not complete without a helper "suitable for him."

Most powerfully, I believe that God needed to demonstrate to Adam, "You are not it." Adam alone was not the complete bearer of God's image, and he was in need of his equal who would complete him, and whom he would complete. Therefore, all power that Adam would exercise toward Eve was designed to be the power to give, and not the power to take. And apart from woman, he was unable to give in a way that completely fulfills the image of God.

Among pagan feminists and other skeptics of the biblical worldview, rooted in real pain, their instinct is that the Bible is the source for male chauvinism, whereas it is quite otherwise. Such feminists have often argued that Genesis 2:18-25 treats women as second-class, or even as an afterthought. But this is because post-biblical and current assumptions are brought to bear on the story. For example, as noted above, the idea of "helper" can be wrongly viewed as subordinate and not equal.

Such pagan feminists have challenged the Genesis text, saying that since Eve was created last, she was therefore an inferior afterthought in the minds of the male chauvinists who are said to have written the story that assumed a male god. But this reading of the text has a foreign concept of chronology and moral order – that somehow the first is best, and the last is least.

In contrast, the whole thrust of Genesis 1 is that God started with the most remote and inanimate portion of the universe, then systematically ordered everything as he moved up to more and more complex life forms, and when all was done, and when the habitat was prepared for the crown of his creation, God made man and woman. But man was not fully male without woman, nor was woman fully female without man.

As well, in the order of creation, Yahweh was always aiming at completion; thus, with the passing days of creation, he repeatedly stated it

36

was "good," as completion was achieved. With Adam in Genesis 2, Yahweh said it was "not good" for him to be alone – goodness was not achieved until the image of God was complete, until woman was made. Woman completed what lacked in man, so that together they equaled mankind. When man and woman were finally standing side by side, as creation was completed, it was "very good."

Another concern raised is the idea that the woman was made from one of Adam's "ribs." Thus, since woman was made from man, it is argued that she must be subordinate and of less worth in the eyes of the biblical writer. However, the language is otherwise. It can be looked at this way: If we had the choice, which would we prefer – to be made from human flesh and bone, or to be made from a pile of dirt? After all, Eve was made from human tissue, and Adam came directly from the dust.

The Hebrew word for "rib" is from *tselah*, which literally means "an aspect of the personality." "Rib" is an accurate word for "an aspect" of Adam's person in physical terms. Eve was made from Adam to indicate her union with him, her complementary equality, with no view to a divisive understanding of woman at war with man that later comes with the fallout of human sin. Whether, in the case of Yahweh forming Adam out of the dust, or of Yahweh forming Eve out of her husband's body, in both cases it involved Yahweh's direct creative action.

Genesis 1:27 identifies their theological union as co-image bearers, and Genesis 2 identifies their physical union as it shows us the order in which they were created to serve the initiative and reciprocity of the power to give. Genesis 2:7 gives us the explicit language of God breathing the breath of life into Adam; and though 2:21-22 does not explicitly say that of Eve, it is implicitly required by the structure of the text. And given the unity of man and woman in their creation in 1:26-28, the same is necessarily assumed.

Eve was an image-bearer, a needed helper for her otherwise incomplete husband, formed by God's direct work, and presented to Adam as a living breathing person. God breathed of his Spirit directly into Eve as he did with Adam. Also, the only difference between the dust of the ground and one of Adam's ribs is that of molecular organization. Men and women are both made from the same stuff of the universe, and we are distinguished from the rest of creation by the image of God breathed into us.

When Adam awoke from his sleep and viewed Eve, we have the first poem in human history. Adam saw his helper, his complement, his equal. And as some like to say, a rough paraphrase of this poem is "Wow!" Adam had just named the animals, and in the process, realized that he was uniquely an image-bearer of God, and that all other creatures were not. The image of God within him – with the gifts of creativity, intelligence, choice, aesthetics and dexterity – needed an equal and complementary partner with whom he also shared these gifts.

Inclusive Spheres of Rule

In the Genesis 1:26-28 passage, Adam and Eve were called to "rule over" the work of creation together, under God and for their joy. In the words "fill and subdue," we see a phrase that defines the inclusive spheres of rule for Adam and Eve. By "inclusive" I mean that God gave to Adam and Eve unique dimensions not replicated in each other, so that true complementarity was possible.

By the same token, there was much overlap in gifts and nature between the man and woman, so that the spheres of rule were not "exclusive" domains. Men and women are equally human, men and women are different, and men and women need each other for a shared humanity. This balance is uniquely provided for in the biblical language; it is the balance of the power to give, to receive what is given, and to give in return.

"Filling and subduing" the earth refers to the dimensions of procreation and to the cultivating of the Garden of Eden to enjoy its fruit, and hence, to cultivate the planet. An inclusive and mutually submissive reality can be seen by the comparison of the muscular strengths between man and woman. The woman's greatest strength is in her cervical and thigh muscles, and that strength is taxed most in pregnancy and childbirth. The man's greatest strength is in his shoulders and biceps, and this strength is taxed most in heavy labor such as moving boulders. A man cannot give birth or natural succor to a child; and a woman cannot, on average, lift nearly as much weight as can a man. But a man can rock an infant to sleep and he can change diapers – as a man. And a woman can do hard and diligent physical labor – as a woman. The distinctives remain.

The complementarity is seen in Genesis 2:7 and 2:22. In 2:7, when God "formed" the man from the dust, the verb employed is *yetzer*. The idea reflects Yahweh as the divine Potter, forming Adam literally from the clay, the red earth, or from the raw materials as it were. In 2:22, when Yahweh "made" the woman from the man's substance, the verb employed is *banah*. Its usual sense is translated as "to build," and contextually the building process here did not begin with the raw materials, but it began with the formed substance already in place. A suitable analogy is to compare the outward building of a house, beginning with the hewing of the lumber from the trees, in the forming of Adam, on the one hand; with the inner finishing of the house, as with beautification details such as furnishings and artwork, in the forming of Eve, on the other.

The word for the human soul ("being" as translated in the NIV) in Genesis 2:7 is *nephesh*. It means that human nature is by definition needful of God's original and continued provisions. His breath provided Adam with his original breath. Also, it means that the human body is a good gift, meant to live forever. Thus, human strength starts with the power to receive and be needful of God's power to give. This term, *nephesh*, rooted in an original needfulness that equals true strength, is crucial for understanding the whole Bible.

In reflecting on *nephesh*, we see the mutual dependency as designed by God. In the order of creation, it was the strength of the man to do the heavy labor, to work as the provider who builds the house and shelters his family from climatic extremes. In the order of creation, it was the strength of the woman in pregnancy, childbirth and succor to build the family that lives in the house. These are inclusive spheres of rule – to "fill and subdue" is a whole unit that requires a whole marriage unit to accomplish it. And when these spheres are honored, all subsequent blessings come. Men work inside the home and women work outside the home in many overlapping functions, but according to their God-given natures, not in contrast to them. (Now, this is a description of the purposes of order of creation, before the entry of human sin, and hence the question of men and women who are single raises important questions for another context).

Right Half and Left Half Sides of the Brain

In the 1980s, research confirmed important biological differences between men and women in their thinking processes. Against certain assumptions of the egalitarianism of the 1970s, Harvard psychologist Carol Gilligan published her influential work in 1982, *In a Different Voice*. It changed the feminist movement with her clinical observations that women think differently than men, and accordingly, models for healthy psychologies cannot be made to apply to girls if the only studies were done on boys – as the reigning psychological paradigm of Lawrence Kohlberg then assumed. Gilligan, despite some good analysis, and in view of Kohlberg's imbalance, said that the problem "all goes back, of course, to Adam and Eve – a story which shows, among other things, that if you make a woman out of a man, you are bound to get into trouble. In the life cycle, as in the Garden of Eden, the woman has become the deviant" (p. 6).

Gilligan's comment about the nature of Adam and Eve and the Garden of Eden is unfortunately the norm among many scholars. Such an assumption then influences those who read these scholars, which translates into the influencing of the cultural elite who determine so much of what assumptions are filtered for the rest of society to hear. Thus, public perception and public policy are affected – many times against the better instincts and common sense of the population at large.

Somewhere in her training, Gilligan accepted an item of biblical eisegesis (a word that refers to placing something into the source, pretending it was there all along, then discovering it later; it is the opposite of "exegesis," which refers to discovering what is truly in the source to begin with). That is, this reflects some woman's interpretation of the text that came not from an understanding of the Bible on its own terms, but from refracting the Bible through the myopia of sin and brokenness. And the chief sin here is that of male chauvinism, where too many girls grew up not seeing the power to give in their father or father-figure, and thus they could not see the power to give in God the Father, and in the biblical witness.

Research began to conclude in the mid-1980s that around the sixth month in utero, the female fetus continues to receive the washing of estrogen over both sides of the brain, whereas the male fetus does not. This discontinuation for the unborn boy allows the right and left sides of his brain to develop distinctly from the point forward, and to operate more independently of each other.

41

The left side of the brain is the locus for analytical, task-oriented, goal-setting and abstract thoughts. The right side is the locus for relational, emotive, concrete and nurturing thoughts. Men and women have both, but this reality of the intrauterine estrogen washing causes significant and necessary distinction. For the man, it enables him to put aside the emotive aspects for a given time in order to concentrate on performing and completing a task. This was necessary for Adam's inclusive sphere to provide for Eve as a husband and as a father to their children. For the woman, she is free from the goal-oriented tasks for the needful season in order to concentrate on the quality of nurturing relationships. This was necessary for Eve's inclusive sphere to provide for Adam as a wife and as a mother to their children. A similar balance between female verbal skills and male spatial thinking reinforces this reality from another angle.

These brain studies confirm what the order of creation assumes, and it is the reversal that subsequently broke the trust of the power to give between man and woman. A woman's "intuition" is in fact a more consistently interactive thinking pattern involving both sides of the brain, always considering relational issues.

In the spring of 1978, my wife, Nancy, and I drove from Pittsburgh to the North Shore of Boston to visit Gordon-Conwell Theological Seminary. As I calculated the 625 or so miles of the trip, I thought in terms of what speed we would average, over what roads, what mileage the Honda Civic would yield, how much it would cost including the tolls on the Mass Pike, where to stop for food and gas, how long to visit with my father in West Hartford, Connecticut, to calculate the estimated time of arrival in South Hamilton, Massachusetts, and to calculate the return trip likewise in order to arrive back at my job on schedule and on budget.

On the other hand, Nancy, then several months pregnant with our first child, was thinking in terms of the Poconos, through which we would travel, along with the many bathroom stops required for the comfort of a pregnant woman. She thought in terms of what nice restaurant we could dine at, and even if we would make it a two-day trip instead of one, and thus, what nice hotel we could find, again, in the Poconos.

It is not that men do not think about relationships, or that women do not think about goals. Rather, men consider relationships through the prism of goal-oriented thinking, and how the successful pursuit of those goals will provide the time, and material well-being, desired for good relationships. And women think of goal-oriented concerns through the prism of the healthy relationships necessary in the process of attaining a goal.

Another way to sum up this balance is to say that the man naturally leads in task-orientation, and the woman naturally leads in relationship building. A mutual submission to this reality leads to healthy marriages and a healthy society. A mutual submission to the power to give.

Three Different Equations for Marriage

Just prior to my 1994 "give and it will be given, or take before you are taken" observation at Smith College, I had said that there are only three possibilities in human relationships, symbolized in three different types of marriage:

100-0;

50-50; or

100-100.

In the 100-0 option, male chauvinism is operative (though female chauvinism can also happen as with Jezebel [read about her in 1 Kings 16:29 - 2 Kings 9:37]). Here the man demands 100 percent and gives nothing. This can also be described as "take before you are taken."

43

The 50-50 option can be described as "egalitarian," and is distinguished philosophically from "equality." In the philosophy of an egalitarian view, the equality of the sexes is defined by an appeal to "sameness." A woman can do anything a man can do, it is said. Accordingly, male and female roles in marriage are said to be interchangeable (apart from the inescapable reality of pregnancy, giving birth and natural succor).

In the "ideal" egalitarian marriage, each partner pursues career goals, careers defined not by service to the home as in a healthy marriage, but careers, which if push comes to shove, take precedence over the home. Thus, cooking and housework are split evenly if they cannot afford a cook or a maid. If and when they have children, maternity leave applies to the man as well as the woman, and they share 50-50 the work of child rearing. With or without daycare or a nanny, the husband is expected to make the same "sacrifice" of time away from his career, as does his wife. Such "sameness," as a definition for equality, is thus supposed to remove culturally impose role distinctions between male and female – and lead to true equality.

However, as the research makes clear, this upper middle-class ideal of egalitarianism is not only a myth, it is also a destroyer of families and children. As many feminists have complained, when they entered such a 50-50 bargain, they discovered that their workloads greatly increased, and their husband's workload remained roughly constant. As women, they were desirous or willing to pursue a career outside the home, but men were, as a rule, unwilling to share the domestic work any more than was otherwise the case (though now, with a culture that has become more thoroughly "feminized," things are more complex). It led to a warfare between one 50 and the other 50. Namely, 50-50 by definition is a taking proposition, with each party having made an idol of career or identity outside of God and family. By putting such an idol ahead of relationship, each party clamored to protect his or her 50 percent. In other words, the arrangement was based on the "right to take" the 50 percent that belonged to him or her, and if one spouse took 51 percent, there was war – the opposite of the power to give.

There is great freedom in a healthy marriage in terms of how income producing work and management of the home are shared, but only when the complementary nature of men and women is affirmed, not when the distinctions are blurred. The irony is that the 50-50 proposition is no different than the 100-0 proposition. It too is "take before you are taken."

The Hebrew word for peace is *shalom*, which primarily refers to integrity and wholeness. The only prescription for social peace is the original one of 100-100 in the Garden of Eden. This is the power to "give and it will be given," where Yahweh Elohim gave 100 percent of his divine best to the human Adam, Adam received the 100 percent and gave 100 percent of his human best to Eve, she received his 100 percent and returned 100 percent of her human best to Adam; then they together, in the integrity and wholeness as husband and wife, gave their 100 percent of their human best in worship to Yahweh Elohim.

This power to give can be seen in the apostle Paul's language concerning mutual submission in marriage (see Ephesians 5:21-33). Wives are to submit to husbands on the one hand, and husbands are to submit their lives as Christ did on the cross on the other hand, which equals a submission to the wife as the nature of leadership rooted in the power to give. Unfortunately, submission is oftentimes a dirty word for people who have been abused by a forced submission rooted in male chauvinism.

The word in the Greek here for "submit" is *hupotasso*, which means, "to place oneself under." People do not want to put themselves under others who will violate them; they do not want to be subject to the power to be taken. We all love backrubs but are lousy at giving ourselves a backrub. The intrinsic nature of a backrub is "to place oneself under" in order to be

45

blessed by another. This is a classic example of the power to give, and only possible as rooted in trust. We all submit to those whom we trust, receiving the power to give as they exercise it; we all recoil from submitting to those whom we distrust, whose purpose is the power to take.

Hence, two choices – give and it will be given, or take before you are taken. I asked Patricia Ireland if she knew of any better arrangement for marriage or the human community. Neither of us can improve upon this arrangement.

Calvin and Hobbes

This issue of giving and taking is reflected in the classic contrast between Swiss theologian John Calvin (1509-1564), and British philosopher and non-theist, Thomas Hobbes (1588-1679). In other words, it comes down to *Calvin and Hobbes* (my all-time favorite comic strip, which was a hall of mirrors and role reversal play on the issues address by the real Calvin and Hobbes).

Hobbes takes as his starting point the reversal, the selfish side of human nature, believing that if there were not a "Leviathan" or monster government to force people away from each other's throats, society would crumble.

Calvin, on the other hand and prior to Hobbes, places faith in the image of God as the origin of human nature in the order of creation, pointing out that society and government cannot exist apart from the qualities of trust. For example, when we buy fish, we automatically trust that it has not been laced with arsenic. If a certain fish market advertised that only "about 1 in 1,000 filets" sold there had toxic amounts of arsenic, what would become of its business? In a thousand ways we give trust in all our relationships, from intimate to casual to distant. We trust, as we drive 60 mph along a country road, that the trucker coming at the same speed the opposite way does not have the sudden urge to cross the centerline. We can come a few feet from death a thousand times every day, all because we trust the broken remains of God's image in others.

If distrust in the social order ever disrupts enough of our daily routines, political anarchy can result, and the invitation for a totalitarian resolution of the anarchy follows (e.g., the French Revolution, the Reign of Terror and Napoleon Bonaparte, in succession). Unless distrust is tethered by biblical ethics in culture, like cancer it can metastasize.

Calvin knew that unless there are those who initiate the giving and nurturing processes, and unless we can trust others to be giving and honorable, then no social order is possible. The quintessential examples are the trust between husband and wife, and the bond of trust between mother and newborn child. Apart from such giving in the family, then in the neighborhood, the local community and on outward, there can be no government.

When examined, it is noticeable that many people who favor expanded top-down government seek out the government as an ersatz family or daddy, oftentimes making up for a deficit in true family units. And most people who favor a limited federal government place more trust in natural family units.

Calvin has assumptions in place that put greater confidence in the *nephesh* of the image of God, in the need for trust, nurture and giving. Such a basis in the image of God gives sober understanding to the sin nature, and therefore the need for checks and balances in constitutional law. Hobbes, having no declared faith in God or in the order of creation and the image of God, becomes existentially enmeshed in a sin nature he theologically denies. His concept of social order predates, but anticipates, the Marxist rights theory that says you must take what you can take to get any rights,

47

and take them from those who oppress you – a prescription for war, sexism, class envy and racial tensions. Calvin reflects the unalienable rights given by the Creator – give and it will be given. It is a prescription for social order, prosperity and peace insofar as attainable this side of the resurrection.

The 100-0 and 50-50 marriage equations are Hobbesian in nature. Only a 100-100 relationship where both parties give 100 percent to each other, with no strings attached, as Calvin recognizes, meets the biblical norm. In view of sinful nature, it is easy to see how the initiative of taking is universal. Thus, a reaction to a reaction only begets further reactive taking, rooted in distrust. We need to be proactive, returning to the image of God and the origins of the power to give in the biblical order of creation, and grasp its trajectory as fulfilled in the order of redemption.

The Babylonian Genesis

In contrast to the biblical Genesis, all pagan origin stories assume the original presence of destruction, and the nature of the human race as a by-product of totally or partially capricious gods, goddesses or spirits. The power to take is assumed from the outset, and it precedes and defines all.

As an example, alluded to earlier, among scholars who are skeptical toward the Bible, the most revered of these stories is the Babylonian Genesis (or *Enuma Elish*). Set forth as the best academic basis to challenge the historical trustworthiness of the Bible, the Babylonian Genesis cannot compare with the three key components of the biblical order of creation. We defined them accordingly:

1. *Yahweh Elohim* (the Hebrew for the LORD God) is the eternal and good Creator.
2. The creation is ordered and good.

3. Man and woman are the crown of God's good creation and made free.

In contrast, the three key components of the Babylonian Genesis are these:

1. *Marduk* (the chief Babylonian deity) is finite and destructive.
2. The creation is rootless, chaotic and evil.
3. Man and woman are a by-product intended for slavery.

The Babylonian Genesis starts with the assumption of a pantheon of time-bound, sexually promiscuous and pre-existent gods and goddesses, engaged in an intramural and an internecine war. A second-level deity at the outset, Marduk, created the universe by killing the chief goddess *Tiamat*, and dissecting her body – splitting it open like a mussel shell, making the heavens with one half of her carcass, and the earth with the other half. He then made the defeated gods of Tiamat's army into slaves, but they complained about this status. In response, Marduk killed his chief remaining opponent, *Kingu*, severed his arteries, and from his blood Marduk created mankind to serve as slaves to the defeated pantheon.

Here we see the assumption of destruction. Mankind has to serve as slaves to the whims and caprice of defeated gods and goddesses, revealing a remarkably low view of man and woman. The Babylonians thought they were bound by the positions of the sun, moon, planets and stars as gods (idolatry and astrology) in mundane and important decisions. They were bound to try and wrest favors from their fatalisms (sorcery), and at the extreme in many related religions, to make human sacrifice to placate the gods – all in an attempt to survive in a hostile universe, as they understood it.

But they also chose this worldview. Is our worth as human beings elevated or trashed by such a view? Do we take joy in a myth that the heavens and earth were made out of a dissected and bleeding carcass of a slaughtered goddess, and that we were made to be slaves to the gods, out of the blood of another dead god? This is Babylon's height.

Babylonian religion starts with the assumption of destruction, then interjects a hope (of carving out survival) that is destined to disappoint, and it concludes with destruction remaining in its dualistic continuity. In other words, the reversal of the biblical Genesis:

destruction → disappointing hope → return to destruction,

versus

creation → sin → redemption.

But, by definition, how can destruction precede creation? Destruction can only destroy what has already been created. The Babylonian "genesis" is a reversal of reality.

An interesting aside in this myth was when Marduk dissected Tiamat's body. The text reads:

The lord rested, examining her dead body,

To divide the abortion (and) to create ingenious things (therewith).

He split her open like a mussel (?) into two parts;

Half of her he set in place and formed the sky (therewith) as a

roof...

(Tablet IV, lines 135-138, translation of Alexander Heidel).

The word "abortion," an act of intrinsic destruction (from the Latin *ab* + *oriri*, "to stop from rising," "to cut off from being born"), is used here to describe Tiamat's corpse. In other words, abortion is viewed as parallel to the corpse of one killed by an act of aggression, and as a means to create the universe. This is the Babylonian Genesis versus Genesis in the Hebrew Bible.

All cultures eventually trace back to Genesis, to Adam's lineage at the first, then through Noah's lineage. As peoples migrated away from Eden, then away from earliest Mesopotamia, and likewise later following Noah's flood, they gradually mixed mythologies in with dimming recollections of God's revelation to Adam about creation.

Their oral traditions and written texts reflected a confusion of creation with destruction, despite their best hopes, since it was the only experience they could judge by. And in a sinful world, with no faithful record of the order of creation at hand, destruction took over – the power to take before being taken. Thus, for reality and hope, for the power to give, it is the biblical order of creation in which we must root ourselves.

Fatherhood and the Power to Give

Around 1994, I met with a minister who was deeply involved in inner-city ministry. He asked me why I focus so much of my attention on "sexual politics." By this he was referring to my concerns for supporting covenantal marriage in the face of debates over human abortion, homosexuality and cognate issues.

He said that issues of drive-by shootings, drugs, poverty and crime were more important concerns. So I asked him if he were familiar with the then recent studies that show some 70-90 percent of men in prison, for crimes against persons or property, were raised functionally, if not completely, without a father or father-figure. He said yes. I then briefly itemized my belief that it is sexual promiscuity, especially in terms of the fatherlessness it produces, which lies at the core of the social evils he rightly is concerned about.

The core of any stable social order resides in the elevation of faithful marriage, and thus "sexual politics" must be addressed first.

Here is the reality: It is the male chauvinism of such sexual irresponsibility that leaves pregnant women and mothers of newborns to fend for themselves – and if the child is not aborted in the womb, he or she is aborted in the power for healthy life choices by the crippling absence of fatherhood.

Fatherless boys thus seek ersatz "families" in the inner cities, which outsiders call "gangs." Without the socializing influence of present and loving fathers, they seek identity with other fatherless boys; and in the ghettos with limited employment opportunities, they easily fall into drug use, then drug selling; and then to protect their "gang" and drug-selling turfs, they buy guns, shoot each other, kill and maim innocent bystanders in drive-by shootings, and thus contribute to social chaos and multiple human misery.

The misery they were given by sexually promiscuous and absent fathers is what they export at large to the culture around them.

And the fatherless girls become sexual adjuncts and toys of the male "gang" members, and/or become prostitutes to support their drug habits. Thus, many die young, forsaken and miserable. And most of this evil can be directly traced back to sexual infidelities, especially in terms of male chauvinisms.

Another way of putting it is to say that the greatest social evils we know can be traced to "the chosen absence of the biological father" – a willful rejection of the power to give on his part.

As I made this argument, I asked the minister (and his theology and politics differed from mine at important junctures): Does abortion-on-demand, the potential legalization of homosexual marriage (and its pre-cognates), laws such as no-fault divorce, and Aid to Families with Dependent Children (AFDC) strengthen or weaken the marriage covenant and family? (AFDC is where, at the time, women and especially teenage girls who would take advantage of it, could get more money from the government to live on if they had children out of wedlock, than if they were married.)

52

Is not the violence in the ghettos traced to a sexually promiscuous male chauvinism in particular? Do not "sexual politics" address the core of this issue? And if we want to address social and racial justice, is not the honoring of the marriage covenant the linchpin? He did not disagree.

In a nutshell, men have a unique point of initiative in the power to give and it will be given, versus the power to take before you are taken.

The Fallout of Abraham Sleeping With Hagar

In Genesis 12-22, the storyline highlights the broken marriage covenant between Abram and Sarai (later renamed Abraham and Sarah). It has led to the greatest of social evils and war in history. It was a unique and unchosen, yet chosen failure of the power to give in fatherhood.

Yahweh had called Abram out of his pagan Babylonian roots to worship the true God. Abram said yes, but he had yet to overcome some pagan assumptions. Yahweh had promised him that even in his and Sarai's old age, they would bear a son, and through Abram's lineage, all the nations of the world would be blessed.

However, Sarai lost patience for the promise to be fulfilled, so she suggested to Abram that he sleep with her Egyptian maidservant Hagar, to "build a family through her" (16:2). Abram foolishly agreed to the idea. This was the power to take from a powerless woman, not the power to give as Yahweh first gives. Sarai sought to fulfill Yahweh's promise by means of human flesh, not by the power of the Spirit. Hagar thus became the first surrogate mother in recorded history, with a rented womb as it were. She was reified, that is, reduced to the status of mere property. For Hagar would not even be allowed, like a pagan concubine, to raise her own child. Rather, Sarai was going to take the child from birth, and Hagar would never hold or breastfeed her very son.

Thus, Hagar despised Sarai when she realized how she was being used. Sarai despised her in return, and the war between the women began. Abram, compromised by sleeping with both women, was impotent to resolve the conflict. He loved his wife, and had erroneously sought to please her intent to build a family through Hagar. But the child Ishmael was also his son, and he loved his son. But because of the war between the women, he was never able to raise Ishmael himself. Sarai made sure of that.

Yet Abraham so loved his son Ishmael that he wanted Yahweh to bless him, and was willing to forego having another son provided for by the power of the Spirit. But Yahweh knew that the human flesh cannot accomplish God's will, and that brokenness had been sown into Ishmael's soul due to the broken marriage covenant and the war between the women.

Ishmael was to turn out as "a wild donkey of a man," always living "in hostility toward all his brothers" (16:12). This was due to being the quintessentially fatherless boy, raised only by Hagar, knowing who his father was, but not understanding why his father was not there for him. It ripped Abraham's soul apart, and he desperately wanted to be Ishmael's present and loving father. He was not choosing to absent himself from Ishmael's life, but due to his prior choice to sleep with Hagar, he now had no choice in the matter if he wanted to love and be faithful to Sarah. So many piercing dilemmas of broken sexuality visit our common humanity. Break the covenant of marriage, and we break the original provision for the power to give.

So Isaac was born to Abraham and Sarah. But the rejected Ishmael hated Isaac as a usurper of their father's love and blessings from the beginning. The war continued between their descendants, that is, the Arabs who come from Ishmael, and the Jews who come from Isaac. The war continues to this day in the Middle East with international consequences, and it is a war that will not be fully resolved until the Second Coming.

In other words, the source for the power to give is in the covenant of marriage between one man and one woman for one lifetime. Any brokenness of this covenant will lead to the power to take. One look at the prevalence of Arab hostility toward the Jews today shows the 4000 years of this history still unfolding – the sons and daughters of Ishmael on the one hand, and the sons and daughters of Isaac, on the other.

Only redemption of the power to give can rescue Arabs and Jews alike, and that power to give is supremely fulfilled by the death of one man on a Roman cross, and the resurrection that followed. The lineage of Jesus traces back to Abraham, and in him all nations will be blessed.

Imagine Ishmael

As a young boy, perhaps five years old.

There he sits outside the small tent, meant to spend these years at play and wonder, yet the intrusion of undeserved pain already gnaws at his soul. There, at the bitter edge of a large nomadic community, he lives alone with his mother Hagar. They are shunned by most people, with furtive glances that young Ishmael doesn't know how to define, but he feels them deeply and unhappily. His mother loves him dearly, holds him tight and teaches him the basics of hygiene, language arts and social skills, of how to grow into manhood.

But his father is not present to model such a manhood, for Abraham is married to Sarah, and Ishmael is the son of a hastily arranged and foolish concubinary with Sarah's maidservant, Hagar. In other words, we come to learn that Ishmael is the son of a discarded slave woman whom Sarah despises for no good cause. Ishmael has no legitimate inheritance rights or honorable standing in the community. He is rejected and feels the shame deeply, all for something that is not his fault, which is not his mother's fault. But at age five, he does not understand these social and sexual realities – he only feels the shame, and doesn't know why he has to feel it, when other boys his age do not. They have daddies at home.

Then imagine the periodic community-wide feast involving perhaps 2,000 people. The seat of honor goes to the patriarch, the wealthiest and most powerful man in the area – Abraham. And next to him sits his beautiful wife, Sarah. Then back at the edges sit Hagar and little Ishmael. Hagar has told him before that this man is his father, but little Ishmael is not allowed to see Abraham, for Sarah would be furious, and they would have to flee for their lives into a desert that only holds death. Ishmael listens, and most of these words are not really understood, but serve as background for the years ahead. At this moment though, the little Ishmael only has one desire – to sit next to his daddy in the sight of all the people, to be honored as daddy's little boy. So simple, not possible, and thus Ishmael grows to be a wild donkey of a man, always fighting for survival and for a dignity and honor not given.

Ibn Ishaq, the first major biographer of Muhammad, claims this lineage for him, and Islam grew out of Arabia 2600 years after Abraham. There is a deep struggle in the subconscious of Ishmael's lineage. The Arabic word for struggle is *jihad*. Underneath the texts of the Qur'an and Hadith this is an inner struggle for honor to erase the undeserved shame, for freedom from a birthright of slavery. It is an inner struggle at the root of the historical and original *jihad* against all who will not submit to Islam. And in the face of this reality, the calling for biblical people is to honor Ishmael, to honor all Arab and Muslim peoples, and all others including ourselves, as equals in the sight of the Creator, Yahweh Elohim, the eternal Father of Abraham, Isaac and Jacob. Only then can the message of the Prince of Peace cut through the boiling tempest of the Middle East – he who was rejected by men as he went to the cross in our stead, then rose from the grave with all rejection conquered. Hagar called Yahweh "the God who sees me," and the name Ishmael means "God hears." Do we also see and hear?

The Chosen Absence of the Biological Father

Far more broadly than the world of Arabia and Islam, there is a universal struggle. The world's greatest social evils are rooted in "the chosen absence of the biological father," whether physical or emotional in nature. And for a broader perspective, see Paul C. Vitz, *Faith of the Fatherless: The Psychology of Atheism.*

If we listen to the children of divorce, we can trace most pain back to what is, or is at least perceived to be such a chosen absence.

If we listen to women forced through an abortion by the chauvinism of irresponsible men, we can trace most of the pain back to such a chosen absence.

If we listen to men and women struggling with issues of homosexual identity or actions, we can trace most of the pain back to such a chosen absence, and likewise for many who struggle with heterosexual promiscuity.

If we look at the emerging soul-searching pain of the children of donor sperm, such a chosen absence is not only deliberate, but mockingly so for perhaps a pittance of cash.

If we look at the poverty in the ghettos of the United States, we can note how at least 70 percent of black children grow up in the pain of such a chosen absence.

If we look at polygamous cultures where sons do not have the chosen full presence of their fathers – in the midst of the sibling rivalries due to the positioning struggles of rival wives – then we can understand people like Osama bin Laden.

Historically, and in a unique way, the pain of such a chosen absence most deeply affects the Arab and Muslim soul tracing back to Abraham and Ishmael. Abraham's absence was chosen yet unchosen. He chose the folly of breaking his marriage covenant with Sarah, at her initiative; but then to keep his marriage intact, yielded to her war against Hagar and Ishmael, yet he never stopped yearning for his son Ishmael, to be a full father to him, but had no power of choice to make it a reality.

How complex broken trust becomes across the pages of history, ever since the original covenant of one man, one woman, one lifetime was assaulted. And only because the Son of God willingly died on the cross for us, splitting the Trinity for some hours in history, yet with unbroken trust in God the Father, and unbroken trust in the power of the Spirit to raise him up from the grave – only because of this calendar defining event, do any of us have hope.

Male Chauvinism and Human Abortion

Back to the forum at Smith College with Patricia Ireland in 1994, the topic that evening was feminism and the Bible. But Patricia raised the question of abortion, and in response, I spoke of human abortion and its male chauvinistic realities.

Namely, the Alan Guttmacher Institute, research arm of Planned Parenthood (owner of the largest chain of abortion centers in the nation) has consistently shown that 82 percent of women who have abortions are unmarried. For the remaining 18 percent, I noted a generalization of what I then knew. But since then, I have itemized more specific data known in Crisis Pregnancy Centers across the nation. They note that of the remaining

18 percent who are married, three-quarters of these women are pregnant through adultery. And of the remaining one-quarter of the 18 percent, most husbands are on their way out the door. In other words, abortions overwhelmingly come from broken relationships where the power to give and receive is not honored by men.

Almost never does a healthily married couple choose to abort their child, unless they believe (wrongly or rightly) that there is serious life or health threats to the mother and/or child. Women get pregnant, and men don't. Sex outside the covenant promises of marriage permits male chauvinism to flourish, in its opposition to the power to give.

At the end of the audience participation time a woman challenged me on how I could respect women's dignity while opposing abortion. We were running out of time, and I only had a few seconds to give answer. I said, "Abortion rips off women as much as it rips off the unborn, and allows male chauvinists to run free." Before I completed these words, the auditorium of some 550 people broke into enthusiastic and sustained applause.

I was astonished. This was not supposed to happen. There I was – a white heterosexual male, an evangelical pro-life minister – six strikes against me on a "politically correct" campus, Smith College no less. The image of God had been touched in these women, and I, as a man, made myself accountable to the power to give. They knew about the male chauvinistic component of most abortion decisions, from direct personal experience, or through the testimony of women friends.

Several years later, I referenced this audience response in a conversation with Patricia. She answered by saying that I had the audience stacked with my supporters. Now, in truth, perhaps 60 to 80 people there were known to be biblically rooted Christians, with the rest being students, faculty or members of the Northampton and surrounding communities. I told Patricia that if I could stack a forum sponsored by Smith College with my supporters, I could also elect virtually all of the U.S. Congress. My power was not rooted in political organization, but in the biblical power to give.

In April 1995, I addressed a Mars Hill Forum at Georgetown University in Washington, D.C., broadcast on C-Span, and my guest as Kate Michelman, executive director of the National Abortion Rights Action League (NARAL). The topic was "Abortion, Blockade and Gunfire: Who are the Peacemakers?" That evening, as Kate had done publicly for years, she decried how her husband left her two-and-a-half decades prior, with three daughters, and as she soon discovered, pregnant. She was impoverished and felt no choice but to have an abortion.

In the forum I identified the greatest violence as that of the male chauvinism that drives the violent reactions of human abortion, the blockade of abortion centers and the gunfire that had percolated in a few instances. Kate knew well the root source violence of male chauvinism. At one point in the evening, as she was beginning to decry the violence of "anti-choice" activists, as she termed it, she suddenly turned to me as we were sitting at a table together, touched me on the shoulder, and said, "Oh, not you John." And the winds of diatribe left her sails.

Human nature is universal. We all seek the POSH Ls of the image of God – peace, order, stability and hope, to live, to love, to laugh, and to learn. The question is whether we seek them on God's terms, or in painful reactions to violations that will never satisfy.

If men were to exercise the power to give a) in chastity before marriage, b) in fidelity within, and c) in the embrace of fatherhood, the debate over "abortion rights" would be nearly nonexistent, restricted essentially to exceptional or hard cases. Most women would carry their child to term, joyfully, if the father were honestly involved and, best yet, as a husband who seeks to model the power to give. There are exceptions, but ones that only prove a larger true generalization.

Homosexuality and the Power to Take Before You are Taken

In the debate over homosexuality and same-sex marriage in the United States, we face the most stringent challenge yet to the intrinsic and universal goodness of man and women in marriage. There is one basic reality underlying this debate, namely, homosexual relationships are by definition incapable of diversity because they are monolithic. Two men in homosexual relationship necessarily reject women in intimate union, and thus they are without complementarity. Two lesbians likewise reject men. The equality and complementarity of man and woman in marriage is the basis for trust and the power to give and receive, and necessary for true diversity in service to unity. Homosexuality is a different reality. There is no sexual complementarity to begin with, thus the power to give as biblically defined has no place of origin.

We cannot honestly address this issue without honoring the image of God in homosexual persons, and in exercising the power to give. In 1988 at Harvard I was taking a course in feminist ethics during my Th.M. studies in ethics and public policy. About two weeks into the term, three women classmates approached me as I was sitting in the cafeteria. One of them introduced herself and her two friends as they pulled up chairs, and she said, "You know John, for an evangelical, you're a nice guy."

She continued, and introduced a topic *de novo*. She noted that the three of them were lesbian, and that every lesbian they knew had been the victim of "physical, sexual and/or emotional abuse" by some man in her early years. These women were in the middle of a large and international nexus of lesbians in the university rich Boston area, and thus this anecdote carried great power (though not being a statistical claim). In only a minority of instances is the biological father implicated in the abuse. Rather it is a stepfather, live-in boyfriend of the mother, some extended family member, or some other man with access to the household who is the usual perpetrator (apart from those who are violated by other teenagers, or adults, as teenagers). In other words, it is usually the result of the chosen absence of the biological father – the absence of the one who was supposed to love, cherish and protect them in the unique power to give of godly fatherhood.

I remember praying in my spirit as I heard these words, *Dear God above, has the church ever heard this? Or do we merely pass judgment on those who are homosexual and move on?* I thought to myself, *These are women for whom Christ died, to offer them the gift of eternal life. How well are we in the church communicating such good news?*

This is also true for boys who grow up in the chosen absence of the biological father. Indeed, it is such male chauvinism that violates boys and girls, and breaks their trust in the possibility of a healthy marriage; and thus, such dysfunction leads to their heterosexual promiscuity and/or homosexuality when they grow up. If men were to exercise the power to give a) in chastity before marriage, b) fidelity within, and c) the embrace of fatherhood, the debate over homosexuality would be nearly nonexistent.

In February, 2004, I addressed another forum at Smith College, with some 500 people, over 300 of whom were avowed lesbians, on the topic: "Is Same-Sex Marriage Good for the Nation?" My guest, Amy Hunt, was a board member of the Massachusetts Gay and Lesbian Political Caucus.

As the forum began, a member of the Smith Christian Fellowship sat among some twenty avowed lesbians (all fellow classmates). They were chortling about how I was going to be chewed up and made ready for shark bait, and they were ready for it. But as the forum progressed, they started to complain about me: "He's being too gracious…"

During the forum itself, I made three observations among others. First, I told the students and others in attendance that I wanted them all to succeed in attaining the fruit of God's image – peace, order, stability and hope, to live, to laugh, to love and to learn. The question is how we best achieve these goals, whether on God's terms, or on our own broken terms.

Second, I stated that I did not want one inch of greater liberty to speak what I believe, than the liberty I first commend to those who disagree with me. The Golden Rule in political context. The Golden Rule, which we will look at more closely later, reflects the essence of the power to give.

And third, I stated that if any homosexual person there happened to be facing danger, and I were in position to take risk and intervene to protect his or her life, I would do so instinctively – simply because that I how I treat all people.

During the question and answer period, one lesbian activist, and one male homosexual activist, both said remarkably similar words – that my opposition to same-sex marriage was "doing violence" to them. I then responded, "Do you mean that I am doing violence to you because I disagree with you?" I could have reversed the moment and said, "Does that mean you are doing violence to me if you disagree with me?" I did not, and had I done so, I could have lost the moment and forfeited the ethics of the Gospel, which is to love those who consider themselves our enemies, and not to accuse them. I could have forfeited the power to give and thus yielded to the power to take when taken.

The fruit of the evening was that the anger level calmed down, opposition was self-muted considerably, thoughtfulness resulted for most in attendance, and the Gospel was tangibly advanced. In fact, one woman came to Christ as a result, and the Smith Christian Fellowship grew substantially in the subsequent months. Many lesbians thanked them for sponsoring the forum, for both sides were heard equally.

The Aggressive Hospitality of the Mars Hill Forums

In 1993, I inaugurated the Mars Hill Forum series, after conceiving of it two years prior. In these forums, I have sought to embrace the same freedom Paul experienced on Mars Hill in Acts 17 (the "Areopagus" in the NIV), where he was spontaneously alone in the presence of perhaps hundreds of the most professionally qualified skeptics possible. He was giving answer for his belief in the good news of Jesus. The Greek term Areopagus (the hill of the god of war, or Ares) referred to the seat of political power in classical Greece. After the Roman conquest, its Latin name, Mars Hill (the hill of the god of war, or Mars) referred to what had thus become a philosophical society.

I seek out the most qualified cultural spokespersons who are skeptics of my understanding of the biblical worldview, and/or its politics, and who wish to pose hard questions. The truth is that skeptics rarely seek out qualified spokespersons of the Gospel to come onto their own turf. So I have sought to exercise the power to give in an aggressive hospitality to their toughest questions in venues of their comfort zone, which as often as possible means a university campus. By "aggressive hospitality" I mean I go out of my way to be in the presence of the questions of skeptics. I am being proactive, not reactive. The power to give. The goal is not to win a debate per se (though facts matter), but in the face of debated issues, to win an honest relationship.

When I first sought funding for these forums, I was speaking with a man who was at a central nexus point for institutional giving within the evangelical church. He loved the idea but told me that the institutional evangelical church would not support it. Why? It is because they would not consent to giving an honorarium to a lead skeptic such as the head of NOW, and thus support such an organization financially. In other words, out of the fear of being taken, there was no vision for the biblical power to give. My convictions were otherwise, consistent with honoring the image of God in all people, and giving honor to the marketplace qualifications of my guests (cf. Romans 12:21; 13:7; 1 Peter 2:17). So I pieced together the forums financially as best I could.

After I moved from pastoral ministry into public policy ministry in late 1983, an elder in my church challenged me. He asked why I was wasting my time on "politics" when I should be preaching the Gospel instead. He maintained that the world was going to hell anyhow, and we should concentrate on "saving souls," not transforming an irreformable culture. Now the Judgment Day will come, but in the meantime, how well will we salt our culture with the good news of the invitation to join the kingdom of God?

I gave him a hypothetical. Imagine if I were to plaster a large state university campus with posters advertising a meeting where I would give a list of evidences for the resurrection of Jesus. How many students would show up? I conducted a scientific investigation in my imagination and concluded that the number would be 35 members of the sponsoring college ministry group, and 2 of their quasi-willing roommates.

But when the power to give is exercised, and genuine hospitality is extended to a qualified skeptic, then one hundred or several hundred students turn out (my experience is largely here in the Northeast and its elite universities where skepticism reigns). The fear of being taken leads to an atrophied and segregated religion; the power to give leads to the intrinsic attractiveness of the Gospel being evidenced in the public arena.

The Power to Give

It is simple: Give and it will be given, or take before we are taken. The covenant of man and woman in faithful marriage is the God-given foundation for the power to give to flourish in any society, and the role of the husband and father is most crucial.

We continually face momentary decisions whether to give or take. We overwhelming yearn for the former, but so often fall into the latter. The only way to grow in the power to give is by seeking God's grace, which is ultimately fulfilled in the person and work of Jesus the Messiah.

♦ ♦ ♦

Chapter Two

The Power to Live in the Light

The Averted Gaze

Have you ever noticed how honest people look you straight in the eyes, and dishonest people will not, choosing instead the averted gaze? Or to put it another way – there are those with nothing to hide and those with much to hide. (Now, this is an observation about western culture as influenced by the Bible; in many other cultures, and in Muslim societies, there are customs where social and sexual distinctions make such eyeball-to-eyeball contact a sign of disrespect – a subject unto itself.)

The averted gaze began with Cain, when he was downcast, avoiding looking at God directly, after having failed to deceive him. We will look at this particular situation later.

On the night before my wedding, in August, 1977, I was picking up a friend at the Pittsburgh International Airport. As I entered the main terminal, a young woman follower of the Hare Krishna sect approached me in her long flowing cotton dress and impoverished look. I was familiar with the sect from previous encounters. She had a bundle of two-day old carnations, and without my permission, she walked up and attempted to pin one to my lapel. The Hare Krishna drill was to then ask you for a donation to an unspecified "children's charity" or such, when in reality it was going to be used to support the sect.

So I instinctively lifted both my hands, palms out, and said, "No thank you. I am a follower of Jesus."

She immediately retorted, "I am a follower of Jesus too." In other scenarios this would have been a great invitation for a theological discussion on who Jesus is according to the Bible, and what a Hindu understanding might be. But I had my friend to meet, and the flight had already arrived.

So I surprised myself by speaking what the Holy Spirit gave me in that moment, "No you aren't." I had never been this bold, nor would I plan this type of response in my mind, presuming to know the status of a person's soul.

When I did, I literally saw a darkness enter her soul and manifest as demons dancing in her eyes. She turned away quickly, uttering a mantra.

Jesus addressed this reality in the Sermon on the Mount:

> The eye is the lamp of the body. If your eyes are good, your whole
> body will be full of light. But if your eyes are bad, our whole body
> will be full of darkness. If then the light within you is darkness, how
> great is that darkness! (Matthew 6:22-23).

The lamp of the body is the window to the soul. A person open to honest communication has eyes full of light, and an eager embrace of life. A person closed to honest or trusting communication has eyes that avoid direct contact, and/or retreat into the shadows of fear. Just as a physician can tell the health of the body's cardiovascular system by looking into the blood capillaries of the eye, so too Jesus is saying there is a deeper spiritual reality that the eyes advertise.

In the Bible, the theme of light versus darkness is a commanding one. It is a theme played out across human history, culture and religion, yet there is only one place where the power to live in the light is fully defined and pursued – the Bible.

Three Domains of Light Versus Darkness

There are three dimensions where light versus darkness play out – physics, ethics and spiritual domains.

The first one is simple, and virtually uncontested. The second one is above reproach, has depths we need to explore, and its grasp leads to the power of an overcoming faith. And the third one is where the contest of the ages finds its crucial focus, where we need as much power as possible.

The Domain of Physics

In the first domain, wherever light is present, by definition darkness cannot exist. Light has an atomic weight, and darkness has none, which means that in terms of physics, darkness does not exist. It is the absence of light. So when the light appears, darkness immediately dissipates. The first words of the Bible, including the first words spoken by God, start with this reality:

> In the beginning God created the heavens and the earth. Now the earth was formless and empty, darkness was over the surface of the deep, and the Spirit of God was hovering over the waters.
>
> And God said, "Let there be light," and there was light. God saw that the light was good, and he separated the light from the darkness. God called the light "day," and the darkness he called "night." And there was evening, and there was morning – the first day (Genesis 1:1-5).

There is an extraordinary amount of detail behind the scenes of Genesis 1:1-5, indeed, in all of the order of creation and the rest of the biblical storyline, in terms of the literary structure of the text, the history of assumptions at play and the technical uses of language in their contexts.

Genesis 1:1-5, and its redemptive parallel in John 1:1-5, are without parallel in human history.

For our purposes here, we can simply say that God makes the universe, not *ex nihilo*, "out of nothing" as it were, for there is nothing outside of God; and like darkness, "nothing" has no independent existence. Rather, the biblical text sets up the act of the eternal Creator who makes what is visible to us out of what is invisible to us (see Hebrews 11:3), that is, from within his comprehensive existence and eternal resources. He forms what was formless until he formed it, he makes the organized out of what was disorganized *(tohu w'bohu* in the Hebrew of Genesis 1:2), he makes the habitable out of what as of yet was uninhabitable, and he calls light into what was theretofore darkness.

The idea of the Creator, Yahweh Elohim – he who is greater than space, time and number – is obviously a concept none of us can wrap ourselves around. Genesis 1:1-5 assumes we know this, so in language we can grasp, we see that God starts the creation of our universe and habitation within it by a statement of physics – God said "let there be light" and there was light.

We know today, through science and the scientific method that sound and light are the very essence of life. This is how the Bible starts – God's voice producing light as the first reality of the physical universe. From astrophysics down to the smallest known particle or wave in the universe, we see the reality of the physics of life. Who could have imagined several decades past the ability to put hundreds or thousands of words on a particle of light, send it half way around the world in a nanosecond, and then be able to download and print it out without any changes in the transfer? Yet worldwide men and women do this every day countless times. When God said, "Let there be light," I can grasp an incomprehensible explosion of energy coming out of his person – the "Hot Big Bang" as it were – as he actively governed its expanse until he had completed our habitat, and then made us in his image to govern it.

These simple physics are assumed throughout the Bible – science and the scientific method. To start with, in Genesis 1:14-19, we read that God makes the sun, moon and stars "to serve as signs to mark seasons and days and years ... to give light on the earth." We see echoes of the power to give, of how the physics of light are given to bless us.

Now too, there is something very powerful happening here in terms of a basis for honest and rigorous science. The word "science" is rooted in the Latin term *scientia*, and it basically means "knowledge." In our era, it carries with it the usual sense of referring to the physical sciences and their study.

The text we have in the Pentateuch, the first five books of the Bible, is also known as the Book or Law of Moses. The history of the text goes back to Adam, but our written copies trace back to Moses as he presented them to the Israelites in the wilderness, circa 1446-06 B.C. Moses was bringing to them the words of God from Adam forward, and in special view of the Israelites becoming a covenant community to live in a land God was giving them. Moses knew well their need to be completely separate from the pagan deities they and their forefathers had encountered back to Abraham and prior.

So he was most deliberate in his choice of language at this point. He did not use the words we would translate as "sun" and "moon," for in other related Semitic and non-Semitic languages, the same words also referred to pagan deities. We know this well today, when we consider the names of our planets, for example, whether it is Mercury as the messenger of the gods, Venus as the goddess of love, Mars as the god of war, or Jupiter as the chief god in the Roman pantheon.

71

Moses wanted no such pagan confusion to be introduced to the Israelites, for all pagan nations worshiped the sun, moon and starry hosts as gods and goddesses. So when Moses identified the sun and the moon as "the greater light" and "the lesser light," he was doing something completely radical – being scientific before being scientific had such an identity. Science is the ability to look at things as they are, and not to succumb to mythology and idolatry. Thus, the physics of light and darkness have a crucial foundation in the Bible, are assumed across it pages, and out of which the ethics and spiritual domains of light and darkness can then be understood.

The Domain of Ethics

In the second domain, the ethics of the averted gaze can be gleaned by looking at two opposite responses to the second coming of Jesus which illustrate the power to live in the light versus the fear of those living in the darkness. In Luke 21:25-28 we see a contrast between apprehension and expectation with respect to the coming judgment on Jerusalem in A.D. 70 and the Second Coming. Jesus commends his disciples to stand up and lift their heads, alluding to the Jewish posture of prayer – standing up, eyes fixed heavenward with arms outstretched to God. Jesus refers to an eyeball-to-eyeball yearning for the soon coming King.

In Revelation 6:15-17, in response to the opening of the sixth seal, the peoples of the earth call on the mountains and rocks to fall on them and "hide us from the face of him who sits on the throne and from the wrath of the Lamb!"

These two snapshots reflect a constant theme in the Bible, where those who live in the light see God as a Friend who will rescue them from judgment; and those who live in the darkness see God as the one who will put on them a wrath they have chosen. The eyeball language is again in place – the unbelievers fear the face of God, and would rather be crushed to dust under the weight of the mountains then to look at Jesus, seek and receive forgiveness.

Do we choose honesty or the averted gaze? In the Sermon on the Mount, Jesus defines the calling for all believers:

> "You are the light of the world. A city set on a hill cannot be hidden. Neither do people light a lamp and put it under a bowl. Instead they put it on its stand, and it gives light to everyone in the house. In the same way, let your light shine before men, that they may see your good deeds and praise your Father in heaven" (Matthew 5:14-16).

To believe in Jesus as Messiah, Lord and Savior, leads inexorably to the power to live in the light. It leads to an unfeigned integrity where our actions are consistent with our profession of faith, where skeptics cannot fault our deeds, and thus their skepticisms melt more readily when they consider who Jesus really is. Jesus calls himself "the light of the world" in John 8:12, and here he calls his disciples the same, where we have nothing to hide, and where we do not embrace a self-righteousness in the process. Christ in us. Do we live in this reality? Jesus was pointedly brutal in confronting hypocrisy, and if we are set free from it ourselves, then as a city on a hill, our faith will be evident and attractive to all truth seekers.

In John 3:16-21, Jesus has been teaching the teacher of the law, Nicodemus, what it means to be born again, and then he followed with language that starts with the power to give, and moves decisively into the power to live in the light:

> "For God so loved the world that he gave his one and only Son, that whoever believes in him shall not perish but have eternal life. For God did not send his Son into the world to condemn the world, but to save the world through him. Whoever believes in him is not

condemned, but whoever does not believe stands condemned already because he has not believed in the name of God's one and only Son. This is the verdict: Light has come into the world, but men loved darkness instead of light because their deeds were evil. Everyone who does evil hates the light, and will not come into the light for fear that his deeds will be exposed. But whoever lives by the truth comes into the light, so that it may be seen plainly that what he has done has been done through God."

John 3:16 is well known in the believing church, and as such its reference to the power to give is readily evident. "For God to loved the world that he gave…" But how often do we read the balance of Jesus' words to Nicodemus? It is ethical, and definitively so.

In other words, belief as defined in the Bible is never separated from the actions that follow from it. In the Sermon on the Mount, Jesus says, in the matter of judging true or false prophets, "by their fruit you will recognize them" (Matthew 7:20). The apostle James hits this concern head on: "What good is it, my brothers, if a man claims to have faith but has no deeds? Can such faith save him?" (James 2:14). James continues with a down-to-earth example of a sterile belief that wishes a man well when he lacks clothes and daily food, versus a living belief that actually seeks to meet his physical needs. The apostle Paul says it is grace – God's gift – that saves us, not works (see Ephesians 2:1-10). But such saving grace, if real, will produce good fruit in the works we pursue. And the key to define true faith is the power to live in the light.

Nicodemus was a member of the Jewish ruling council, the Sanhedrin, and thus he had great power, influence and stature. Yet due to his fear of his fellow Pharisees and others who lived ethically and spiritually in the dark as they opposed Jesus, he came to Jesus at night. He was seeking Jesus – he was seeking to live in the light, but still trapped in darkness. So Jesus took advantage of the physics of the nighttime darkness at play and stated the ethics of his coming into the world.

Namely, Jesus came not to condemn, but to save. Condemnation is the nature of the devil, "the accuser," the prince of darkness. And Jesus came to set us free from the devil's condemnation and the condemnation we also pull down on ourselves, and others, by believing the devil's lies. Jesus then says that belief in him will save us from condemnation, but that those who do not believe are condemned already because their unbelief is chosen, and accordingly Jesus shows that it is a matter of living in the light versus living in the darkness.

For anyone who lives in the light, and pursues it consistently, we have nothing to fear from those who live in the darkness – for in the depths of their souls, they live in fear of being exposed, always looking over their shoulders. We have no fear, desiring for all people, in the sight of God, to see our actions, to glean our motivations toward all people. For example, it has long been my practice never to speak of someone away from my presence any differently that I would if they were with me, face to face.

I have discovered repeatedly, in the midst of deep clashes over theological and political issues in our culture, that if I live in the light, those who want the same – no matter how much we might otherwise disagree – will respond favorably. Those who are committed to living a lie for the sake of self-aggrandizing power, of the power to take before being taken, will avoid contact with me as much as possible.

Does this mean I have a power of self-righteousness? By no means. Rather, it is a power of unfeigned humility that I pursue. In his first epistle, the apostle John gives these words:

> This is the message we have heard from him and declare to you:
> God is light; in him there is no darkness at all. If we claim to have
> fellowship with him yet walk in the darkness, we lie and do not live

by the truth. But if we walk in the light, as he himself is in the light, we have fellowship with one another, and the blood of Jesus, his Son, purifies us from all sin.

If we claim to be without sin, we deceive ourselves and the truth is not in us. If we confess our sins, he is faithful and just and will forgive us our sins and purify us from all unrighteousness. If we claim we have not sinned, we make him out to be a liar and his word has no place in our lives (1:5-10).

I seek to grasp this in the depth of my soul. Or as the apostle Paul puts it in a different context, "Let God be true, and every man a liar" (Romans 3:4). Apart from God's grace, we are all readily tempted to lie when self-preservation is at stake, minimally, and from there its cancer can grow into aggressive lying. And every biblically faithful Jew or Christian knows this.

Thus, the apostle John hones in on such a reality as he purges hypocrisy. If we say we have fellowship with God, who is light, then we can have no darkness in us – and the nature of darkness, rooted in ignorance and/or fear, is to lie, to deceive, to break the Ninth Commandment: "You shall not give false testimony against your neighbor" (Exodus 20:16). The power to live in the light is the power to be a truth teller, and truth telling begins with candor about the sin nature and the need to depend on God's grace given in the Messiah.

Thus, the power to live in the light yields a remarkable freedom. God does not call us to be sinless, for that is not possible until we are clothed with the resurrection body at the Last Day. But God does call us to be blameless, and the way to be blameless – that is, "purified" from all unrighteousness – is for us to candidly and humbly confess our sins daily, even moment by moment. Then our sins are removed, we are free, we have nothing to hide, and the good news can be seen in us, even in spite of ourselves. The greatest charge against Christians is that of hypocrisy, as

Jesus leveled it against the orthodox religious elitists of his day. The power to live in the light delivers us from such a charge, and this is a power that the devil cannot mimic or touch. Indeed, the devil's only power to touch us is at places where the darkness of ignorance, fear or dishonesty and rebellion, are still present within (see 1 John 5:18).

The Domain of Spiritual Territory

In the third domain, this leads us back to John 1:1-5, and its deliberate and remarkable parallel to Genesis 1:1-5:

> In the beginning was the Word, and the Word was with God, and the Word was God. He was with God in the beginning.
>
> Through him all things were made; without him nothing was made that has been made. In him was life, and that life was the light of men. The light shines in the darkness, but the darkness has not understood it.

Thus, just as God's first words in Scripture are "Let there be light," here we see that Jesus as the Word is the "light" – defining John's constant theme of light versus darkness. The physics and ethics are in place in this parallel between Genesis and John, and now we are introduced to the spiritual war between light and darkness.

In v. 5, as the light shines into the darkness, the NIV says that the darkness has not "understood" the light. In physics, we see this, as darkness does not atomically exist and it dissipates in the presence of light. Darkness is by definition the absence of light, a nothingness. In ethics, we see that those who by choice live in the darkness want nothing to do with the light out of their fear of being exposed to truth, reality and accountability.

Yet the Greek term in place for "understood" in John 1:5 is far more dynamic yet – *katalambano*. It means to reach up, seize, pull down, dethrone and trample – to conquer. Thus, another translation here is that the darkness has not "overcome" the light. Or to flesh it out a little more, we cannot overcome what we do not understand. In war, we need to know the enemy better than they know themselves if we are to be assured of victory, and this is more so in the world of spiritual warfare. Darkness cannot know or comprehend the light, and light knows that darkness will flee its presence by definition of terms. Satan is the prince of darkness in the face of Jesus who is the Light of the world, and thus he cannot understand and overcome Jesus. Period. He is, literally, the "prince of nothing." The only way the devil can harm believers is to the extent we allow any darkness to remain in us – whether rooted ignorance, fear or rebellion.

Sorcery at the Right Hand of Power

There is a commanding theme across the biblical storyline, what I call "sorcery at the right hand of power." It is the defining reality of the purposes for spiritual warfare, and it all comes down to a contest between the Light and the darkness.

In Genesis 3, the devil disguises himself as a serpent and successfully tempted Adam and Eve to eat the forbidden fruit – thus bringing death into the human experience. Before Yahweh Elohim explained what the curse of disobedience would do to the man and woman, he first cursd the ancient serpent:

> Cursed are you above all the livestock
> and all the wild animals!
> You will crawl on your belly
> and you will eat dust
> all the days of your life.
> And I will enmity

between you and the woman,

and between your offspring and hers;

he will crush your head,

and you will strike his heal (vv. 14-15).

To properly understand the origin and nature of Satan and the demons, it requires a grasp of the whole biblical storyline, for there is no formal "demonology" in the Bible. That is, there is no systematic and chronological explanation of the devil's history and nature. That task is well beyond our purview here, but the reason for no formal demonology comes down to a simple reality of light versus darkness. In the preface to his masterful little allegory, *The Screwtape Letters*, C.S. Lewis says: "There are two equal and opposite errors into which our race can fall about the devils. One is to disbelieve their existence. The other is to believe, and to feel an excessive and unhealthy interest in them. They themselves are equally pleased by both errors, and hail a materialist or a magician with the same delight."

If we have an unhealthy interest in the devil's nature and machinations, we will have been seduced. Precisely to protect us from such a temptation, the Bible only shows Satan's nature as the darkness being scattered by the light. The light defines all; darkness defines nothing. So if we know the Light, we know and overcome the darkness. Thus, in the Bible, the devil and his troops only show up when in contrast to the light that exposes them, and from which they flee. And in this storyline we grasp that the devil was initially a cherub, a high-ranking angel, who chose to rebel against God, and hence lost his position and descended into darkness.

In the Garden of Eden, Satan was too cowardly to show up, in the light, and announce his identity to Adam and Eve. So he veiled himself in proxy, through a member of the animal kingdom, a serpent. Then the curse prophesied a war between the ancient serpent's offspring and that of the woman. Yet as a fallen angel, Satan could have no real offspring; all he could do was seduce and kidnap human beings into being his children, a theme Jesus hit hard with certain Pharisees. The singular male offspring of Eve proved ultimately to be the Messiah, who in his atoning death crushed the ancient serpent's head and then rose from the grave with all power.

Thus, Satan feared the coming Messiah, and his strategy from that point forward was to kill the seed of the woman so the Messiah would not come and pronounce final judgment on him. The devil tried to do this by proxy as he got Cain to kill Abel. Cain proved to be the devil's lineage, his first kidnapping victim, and he murdered Abel, who was the initial seed of the faithful lineage from Adam. Then, Yahweh raised Seth up to replace Abel. From this point forward, the Bible traces the lineage of the messianic remnant until Jesus appeared, and critically, against a backdrop of the devil's lineage which was seeking to wipe them out. The devil seeks liars and murderers to gain high political positions of power, so as to oppose the religious, political and economic liberty of people to see the Gospel lived, hear it proclaimed, and thus believe in it.

This covers huge biblical territory. But for our purposes here, let's look at some crucial junctures where the good news was opposed by sorcery at the right hand of power, where the darkness relentlessly sought to dethrone the Light.

Noah, Babylon and Abraham

The ancient serpent almost succeeded twice in killing off the messianic lineage. First we see this with Noah (in Genesis 6-9), where only one family on the planet remained faithful to Yahweh Elohim as the true Creator. Wickedness was rampant, and Yahweh brought judgment.

And as civilization began to grow again, the Babylonian culture came to pass as rooted in the Tower of Babel. This tower was a ziggurat in service to astrology. Astrology is the belief that the sun, moon and stars are pagan deities, and these deities are capricious, not friendly, to people, unless a bargain is struck. Without such a bargain, people are consigned to suffer the "fates" of what the gods and goddesses will do to them.

The sorcerer is the pagan priest who seeks to strike these bargains on behalf of his clients, and some sort of sacrifice is called for – whether a modest grain offering, or something as extreme as human sacrifice. When pagan people suffered from floods, drought, poor crops, war, disease, infertility, etc., they believed it was due to having somehow displeased these gods and goddesses. Thus they would make the offering or sacrifice the sorcerer would dictate to avoid such fates. Babylonian religion is thus the original pagan religion, and it is a plague on humanity until its final destruction in Revelation 18.

This growth of pagan religion almost snuffed out the messianic remnant a second time. Abraham's father, Terah, was a Babylonian idolater (see Genesis 11:31-32; Joshua 24:2), and Yahweh called Abraham out of Ur of the Chaldeans (southern Babylonia) to Canaan. Abraham was likely the only non-syncretist man still living (apart from Melchizedek and his unique nature). A "syncretist" is someone who seeks to mix opposing realities, in this case, pagan gods with the true God – a sin Israel and Judah fell prey too, leading up to the Assyrian and Babylonian conquests.

Another way of putting it today is with the phrase "All paths lead to the same God." They do not. But from all paths God calls people to himself. From the era of Babylon on forward in the Bible, pagan religion sought to reduce the true God, Yahweh Elohim, down to the level of false gods. So for the pagans of Abraham's day, Yahweh was just another god. But Abraham said no.

Abraham was thus the last man in the faithful lineage, and Yahweh promised him a son through whom all nations would be blessed. This proved to be Isaac, and the lineage down to Jesus continued. But the family of Isaac, beginning with his grandson Joseph, was to suffer 400 years of undeserved slavery in Egypt before the Exodus – the defining identity for the Israelites. Their rescue was led by Moses.

Joseph and Pharaoh

In Genesis 37-50, we have the remarkable saga of Joseph's life. From his youth he was gifted in dreams, but this sparked envy among his ten older brothers, who when the opportunity came, sold him into slavery. Joseph ended up in Potiphar's household, the captain of the guard for Pharaoh, king of Egypt. He prospered, was put in charge of all Potiphar's household, only to be slandered by Potiphar's lustful wife, and thus thrown into prison.

But there he prospered again, being put in charge of the prison by the warden. He accurately interpreted the dreams of two of the Pharaoh's imprisoned servants, the chief baker (who was later hanged) and the cupbearer (who was later restored to his position). Sometime thereafter, Pharaoh himself had two disturbing dreams. His response was to send "for all the magicians and wise men of Egypt" (Genesis 41:8), but they were unable to interpret his dream.

These were the classical "sorcerers at the right hand of power," appearing briefly here and for the first time in the Bible. But given their inability to interpret the dreams, the chief cupbearer spoke of Joseph, and Pharaoh summoned him. Joseph gave interpretation through God's power, and this led to Pharaoh appointing him second-in-command over the nation.

Thus, Joseph's sufferings led him to be in place to rescue his father's family, and thus the Messianic lineage, and likewise Egypt and the

Pharaoh, from the forthcoming famine. Godly counsel at the right hand of power triumphed over sorcery, yet the devil was relentless, as Joseph's progeny ended up being enslaved by subsequent pharaohs for 400 years.

Moses and the Egyptian Sorcerers

When Moses first attempted to rescue the Israelites from Pharaoh's enslavement, he did so an act of murder, and had to flee for his life (see Exodus 2:11ff). Forty years later, when Yahweh called him to do it by the power of the Spirit, the humility of his exile allowed him to be used of the Lord. His confrontation turned out not to be a matter of human strength – as though he could raise up an army to overcome Pharaoh's military might. No, the contest was in the spiritual domains, in the war between demons and godly angels. And the means of the devil is to have proxies, most particularly, sorcerers at the right hand of power.

Pharaoh was supported by such occultic power, and this was the real battle Moses faced. The first time Moses and Aaron confronted Pharaoh with the words from Yahweh, "Let my people go" (Exodus 5:1), the whole conflict was handled in terms of human strength – Pharaoh multiplying the workload for the Israelites. The second time, the spiritual contest was engaged. In Exodus 7:8-13 the Egyptian sorcerers mimicked a miracle performed by Moses and Aaron, making their staffs become snakes – but the staff of Aaron swallowed up their staffs.

Though Aaron's staff was superior, we see how Pharaoh relied on the wise men, sorcerers and magicians (all referring to the interfacing names describing counselors trained in pagan religion and occultic power). This is sorcery at the right hand of power, where the devil has one defining goal, namely, the killing of the messianic lineage. The word "occult" means that which is hidden or obscured, that which is not in the light; and that is

83

exactly the nature of the "secret arts" of the Egyptian magicians (see Exodus 7:11 for the introduction of this term).

In their fifth visit to Pharaoh in Exodus 8:16-19, we have the last stand of the occultic power, where the Egyptian sorcerers could not mimic the miracle performed by Moses and Aaron. They had to say to Pharaoh, "This is the finger of God."

Yet despite the obvious superiority of Yahweh and his delegates, the devil was unrelenting in his agenda. He directly and indirectly sought to influence political leaders in order to kill the messianic lineage. They lived in the darkness, and they relied on secret arts or secret counsel in order to oppose the good.

The Saga of Bala'am

In Numbers 22-24, Balak, king of Moab, sought to use sorcery to curse Moses and the Israelites during their exodus from slavery in Egypt. He sent emissaries to Bala'am, a sorcerer from Babylon, offering him "the fee for divination." Balak and Bala'am were syncretists, viewing all gods as local and tribalistic in nature, and that through divination, these gods could be manipulated for venal purposes.

Bala'am treated the God of Israel this way, but God would not be manipulated, and told him not to curse Israel. Thus Bala'am refused Balak's initial offer. But Balak then sent more distinguished emissaries, with a greater financial lure. Here Bala'am resorted to his manipulative ways of sorcery, seeking to see "what else" Yahweh might say.

In Genesis 18, Yahweh allowed Abraham to repeatedly intercede on behalf of those in Sodom and Gomorrah, in a conversational reality of how Yahweh treats us as image bearers of God, created to govern wisely. Bala'am was at the other extreme in his purposes, yet too he was given the same freedom in Yahweh's sight. Thus, to educate Bala'am in the truth, God affirmed Bala'am request and allowed him to go with the emissaries, "but only do what I tell you."

However, as Bala'am departed the next morning, he was opposed by the angel of Yahweh, whom he did not see, but whom his donkey saw. And here we read the famous story of Yahweh speaking through the donkey to restrain the sorcerer's recklessness. Namely, we reap what we sow, and we may press the Lord for something, which he gives us only to show us reality and hopefully lead us to repentance.

So Bala'am was able to continue on. But in each of the three times he tried to curse Israel in Balak's presence, Yahweh only allowed him to bless Israel more each time. Balak was furious, Bala'am then gave another oracle that promised the Messiah, followed by oracles concerning the Amalekites and Kenites. He then went "his own way" without any payment.

However, even though Yahweh restrained Bala'am and reversed Balak's intention to curse Israel, the sorcerer did not trade in his old ways. He then gained his income by organizing a strategy to seduce the Israelite men by Moabite women into sexual promiscuity and idolatry (see Numbers 25:1ff in concert with 2 Peter 2:15 and Revelation 2:14).

The Saga of Ahab and Jezebel

Between 1 Kings 16 and 2 Kings 19, we have the remarkable saga of Ahab and Jezebel. Following Israel's rebellion against Solomon's son Rehoboam (see 1 Kings 12), the Israelites were divided into the southern and northern kingdoms. The southern kingdom was known as Judah, with the capital of King David's city, Jerusalem. The northern kingdom was known as Israel, with the capital of Samaria. Among the kings of the north, most were unfaithful to the Law of Moses, and increasingly so.

The Assyrians destroyed the northern kingdom in 721 B.C., all the people were scattered among the Gentile nations, and among their descendants were the Samaritans. Among the kings of the south, many were unfaithful to the Law of Moses, but some were faithful or very faithful. And following the destruction of Jerusalem and Judah by the Babylonians in 586 B.C., the remnant of the remnant were the Jews (Judahites), out of whom Jesus came.

Ahab was a northern king, and he is introduced in 1 Kings 16:28-33 as more evil than his father. He married a pagan queen, Jezebel, who led him to worship the Canaanite god Ba'al.

As Yahweh instructed Moses, the reason for the existence of Israel was its nature to be a nation "set apart' (the meaning of the word "holy") to God, and thus set apart from pagan nations and pagan religion which only polluted the truth with their devotion to sorcery, sacred prostitution and, at the extreme, child sacrifice.

Thus, it was a great evil for Ahab to marry a pagan queen, who turned out herself to be a sorceress, guilty of "witchcraft" (see 2 Kings 9:22). The devil was working on the destruction of the messianic remnant, and here by bringing sorcery to the right hand of power in the person of Jezebel.

Yet the Lord always sends his prophets to provide godly counsel at the right hand of power. This is what Moses offered Pharaoh. And in the days of Ahab and Jezebel, Yahweh sent many prophets to hold Ahab accountable, especially Elijah.

Jezebel's influence is seen in 1 Kings 18 as she had an agenda to "kill off the LORD's prophets," and yet Obadiah, who served in the court of Ahab, rescued 100 of these prophets at his own risk. In the storyline that follows, Elijah's counsel was rejected by Ahab, except momentarily, when he got scared. Elijah was the thorn in the side to Jezebel. He challenged the 450 pagan prophets of Ba'al, and the 400 pagan prophetesses of Asherah "who eat at Jezebel's table." In other words, these were 850 sorcerers in service to a lead witch who manipulated the king of Israel. Sorcery at the right hand of power.

Elijah was powerfully successful in this challenge, as Yahweh showed up in miraculous power on Mount Carmel. Yet afterward, when Jezebel threatened to kill him, he fled. The devil is the prince of darkness, so how and why did the prophet of the light flee darkness? Only because Elijah believed a lie, which is to say, allowing some darkness of fear to enter his soul. Whereas darkness by definition has no existence and power, we give it power when we do not live fully in the light ourselves.

As the story unfolds, Jezebel urged Ahab onto great evil, Elijah rebuked him, and Ahab repented briefly. But then he refused the counsel of Yahweh's prophet, Micaiah, and this led to his death. Jezebel outlived Ahab, but ultimately died an ugly death of her own doing.

Saul and the Witch at Endor

From the time of Joshua, the successor of Moses, Israel was led by a series of judges. They were local men (or a woman in the case of Deborah) who followed the Law of Moses where Yahweh was King. Among the judges there were those who were faithful to Yahweh and the Law, and those who were unfaithful. The final judge was Samuel, the epitome of a good judge like Joshua. But his sons squandered his leadership, and in the vacuum, Israel started to call for a human king in the pagan sense.

Thus, they rejected Yahweh, and Saul became king. He proved venal and self-serving, but he did rid Israel of all the mediums and spiritists consistent with the Law. Then, near the end of his life, he was fearful of the Philistine army, he had been repeatedly rebuked by Samuel before his death, and also rebuked by David's example. The gathering storm of judgment was approaching his soul, he had walled himself off from hearing from

Yahweh, and in his desperation he disguised himself and sought out a medium, a witch, looking for advice on how to keep his political power (1 Samuel 28).

He found a witch in Endor who was in hiding from his edict. She was fearful, but heeded Saul's to call up Samuel. When Samuel showed up, by Yahweh's intervention, the witch shrieked. She knew her ruse was foiled (not expecting the real Samuel to show up), she realized who Saul was, and in the end Samuel rebuked Saul again. In other words, Saul rebuked sorcery at the right hand of power initially, but he also rebuked Yahweh's prophet, and at his desperate end, used sorcery to try and call for Samuel's help beyond the grave. Saul's death soon followed – sorcery at the right hand of power does not bring life.

Daniel and the Sorcerers of Babylon

The book of Daniel is remarkable in many ways. The devil was delighted that the city of Jerusalem, its temple to Yahweh and the remnant nation of Judah, were under assault by the Babylonian empire prior to and especially from the beginning of King Nebuchadnezzar's reign in 605 B.C. The complete destruction occurred in 586 B.C. In 605, he deported a portion of the Judahite nobility to Babylonia, "young men," with the purpose of training them in the religion, culture and politics of Babylon. The relentless demonic war against the messianic lineage continued.

Daniel and his three friends, Hananiah, Mishael and Azariah (better known by their given Babylonian names, Shadrach, Meshach and Abednego) were among those deported. They excelled, especially Daniel, in all they did, maintaining fidelity to the Law of Moses while learning "all kinds of literature and learning" (1:17). This would have included the practices of sorcery. In other words, they were gifted to learn about the

88

"secret arts" of pagan religion, and yet they were not seduced by it. Indeed, as light dispels the darkness, they were in control, even though they were slaves.

But as it turns out, these slaves – through Yahweh's redemptive power to use human weakness in the face of demonic strength – ended up in high ruling positions within Babylon, helping to preserve the messianic remnant.

In chapter 1, Daniel and his friends won the favor of their captors. In chapter 2, when the "magicians, enchanters, sorcerers and astrologers" could not reveal and interpret the king's dream, they behaved like sycophants, desperately clinging to their elitist positions, their positions of sorcery at the right hand of power:

> The astrologers answered the king, "There is not a man on earth who can do what the king asks! No king, however great and mighty, has ever asked such a thing of any magician or enchanter or astrologer. What the king asks is too difficult. No one can reveal it to the king except the gods, and they do not live among men."
>
> This made the king so angry and furious that he ordered the execution of all the wise men of Babylon. So the decree was issued to put the wise men to death, and men were sent to look for Daniel and his friends to put them to death (2:10-13).

This brief profile tells us much. First, the pagan sorcerers knew they were living a lie, and Nebuchadnezzar knew it too. In view of his disturbing dream, he wanted them to interpret it. So they said yes – but because he knew they were pretenders, trying to "gain time" and mislead him, he required them first to tell him what the dream was. This required supernatural gifts, and here they became desperate. Their "gods" were nothing more than the deceptions of demons, and whereas they might have known some demonic power, they could not mimic the real thing as the Egyptian magicians also learned.

Second, Daniel and his three friends were not among these "magicians, enchanters, sorcerers and astrologers" at the time Nebuchadnezzar made the demand. Yet, we see how highly valued they were to the king before this matter arose:

> At the end of the time set by the king to bring them in, the chief
> official presented them to Nebuchadnezzar. The king talked with
> them, and he found none equal to Daniel, Hananiah, Mishael and
> Azariah; so they entered the king's service. In every matter of
> wisdom and understanding about which the king questioned them, he
> found them ten times better than all the magicians and enchanters in
> his whole kingdom (1:18-20).

In other words, though their wisdom far exceeded that of the pagan "wise men," and as the rest of the book of Daniel indicates, they were never accepted as social equals – and no surprise. They knew pagan religion inside out while maintaining fidelity to the Law of Moses, and this was not acceptable to petty sycophants, or to the ancient serpent orchestrating this sorcery at the right hand of power.

And third, when Daniel and his friends learned of the decree, they acted with "wisdom and tact" and convened an intercessory prayer meeting (vv. 14-23). God then gave Daniel the answer in a night vision, and he revealed it to the king, not in the power of human ego and ability, but in giving all praise to God. In so doing, Daniel and his three friends also saved the lives of the pagan sorcerers who deserved death – the very nature of the power to give. They served as true prophets at the right hand of power, directly rebuking the sorcerers at the right hand of power.

Then the king placed Daniel in a high position and lavished many gifts on him. He made him ruler over the entire province of Babylon and placed him in charge of all its wise men. Moreover, at Daniel's request the king appointed Shadrach, Meshach and Abednego administrators over the province of Babylon, while Daniel himself remained at the royal court (2:48-49).

Even though their lives were spared, this infuriated the pagan "wise men." Thus, in chapter 3, they were quick to accuse Shadrach, Meshach and Abednego when they refused to bow down to the pagan image set up by Nebuchadnezzar, making them liable to death in the blazing furnace. And who knows how the "wise man" plotted for Nebuchadnezzar to set up the image to begin with, and demand all people to bow down to it – as in chapter 6, similar enemies of Daniel misled King Darius to issue a decree by which they intended to ensnare Daniel and have him executed.

The three young Jewish men trusted God, spoke the truth to the king, and were rescued from the furnace by an angel of God. And when they came out of the fire, we see a remarkable scene:

> So Shadrach, Meshach and Abednego came out of the blazing furnace, and the satraps, prefects, governors and royal advisers crowded about them. They saw that the fire had not harmed their bodies, nor was a hair of their heads singed; their robes were not scorched, and there was no smell of fire on them (3:26-27).

Imagine all the sycophantic elitists crowding around the three men, unable to grasp power of which they knew not, yet hoping, perchance, for something to cling to – a singed hair, a smell of smoke on their clothes. And here we see the power of light versus darkness – the servants of the darkness could not understand and overcome servants of the Light.

In chapter 4, Daniel again interpreted a dream for the king, one that led to his judgment. During King Nebuchadnezzar's seven-year exile of madness, demonically driven no doubt, Daniel the slave became the de facto ruler of the Babylonian empire. Here we see the reversal of the reversal, the power to give and the power to live in the light overtaking the power to take and the power of the occult. And as a result, Nebuchadnezzar repented of his sins and proclaimed Daniel's God to be the true God.

This is but a brief overview of a central theme in the book of Daniel, further highlighted by the demonic powers behind political evil (see the "prince of Persia" and "prince of Greece" language in 10:13,20) – the contest between light and darkness, between sorcery at the right hand of power and God's power to raise up godly counsel at the right hand of power. In the United States today, or in other nations too, how many truly Spirit-filled counselors or prophets are even known to those in high political power? Who in the church would be called on today as Nebuchadnezzar called on Daniel?

Esther, Mordecai and Haman

The relentless war of the devil against the messianic lineage continued. In the book of Esther, ca. 460 B.C., about 80 years after the end of the Babylonian empire and some 70 years after the passing of Daniel, the devil attempted to wipe out all the Jews in the Medo-Persian empire (which meant almost all of Jewry at the time), again through a chosen proxy.

The story begins with how Yahweh raised up godly counsel at the right hand of power – as a Jewess named Hadassah, who went by her Persian name Esther, became queen, the wife of King Xerxes. Her cousin Mordecai raised her after her parents died.

Mordecai, who held a high position in the civil service, overheard an assassination plot against the king, and informed Esther. The plot was foiled, and Mordecai's role was recorded "in the book of annals in the presence of the king" (2:23).

Yet in an apparent disjunctive, King Xerxes thereafter elevated a previously unknown man, an Amalekite named Haman, to "a seat of honor higher than that of all the other nobles" (3:1). The king then commanded all his officials to bow down to Haman, but Mordecai, a Jew who knew the history of the Amalekite attempt to wipe out the Israelites during the Exodus, refused to do so. This Amalekite attempt was part of the devil's unrelenting agenda. In the face of Mordecai's continued refusal, Haman became enraged and learned that Mordecai was a Jew.

Accordingly, Haman directly influenced King Xerxes to set into motion an extravagant plot to kill all the Jews in the kingdom. Sorcery at the right hand of power. Mordecai was mortified with the news and counseled Esther to risk her life and appeal to the king. This Esther did with great tact and wisdom and succeeded in gaining the king's favor. The result was that Mordecai was publicly honored, Haman's plot was reversed, the edict to kill the Jews was thwarted, Haman was hanged on the gallows he had prepared for Mordecai, his estate went to Esther, and Mordecai was given Haman's office. Thus, we witness the reversal of the reversal and the establishment of godly counsel at the right hand of power. The messianic lineage was protected.

Jesus, in the Face of His Enemies

Jesus was consistently stalked and plotted against by his sworn enemies – Jewish leaders who became de facto children of the devil – the quintessence of sorcery at the right hand of power. This I look at in my book, *Jesus, in the Face of His Enemies*.

Paul, a Jewish Sorcerer and a Roman Governor

In Acts 13:1-12, we read of another conflict between a servant of the Light and sorcery at the right hand of power, as Barnabas and Saul (soon to go by his Roman name, Paul) traveled to Cyprus preaching the Gospel. They were invited to an audience with the proconsul (governor), Sergius Paulus, who was "an intelligent man." But they were opposed by a Jewish sorcerer (an oxymoron), Bar-Jesus, also known as Elymas.

In this conflict, Paul identified Elymas as "a child of the devil," that is, the offspring of the ancient serpent in Genesis 3. Thus we have great evil at play, where Elymas had forsaken the God of Israel, sold his soul to the devil, and has wormed his way into being the attendant, the right hand man to the Roman governor of Cyprus. So often, as human history shows, the power behind the throne is what drives public policy – as we have foundationally seen in the biblical profile of Jezebel and the Babylonian sorcerers.

Elymas tried to turn the governor away from the faith. The reputation of Barnabas and Paul preceded them, and Sergius Paulus wanted to hear the Gospel. It is reasonable to assume that what the governor did was to instruct Elymas to invite Paul and Barnabas to his home. Elymas thus twisted between a need to obey his boss' order, while at the same time trying to dissuade him from becoming a Christian.

We can imagine Paul and Barnabas standing there in a formal reception, with Elymas standing next to the governor, trying to give him – by body language, hints or explicit words – reasons to reject the Gospel. Then the explosion of light into the sorcerer's dark world.

Paul would have none of it. He spoke in the power of the Lord and told this proxy deceiver that he would be blind for a season. When light is too bright for our mortal frames, we become blinded. And for Elymas this was also an act of mercy. He was explicit in his opposition to the truth, and now his blindness tested his misplaced faith. His chosen spiritual darkness now became a physical blindness. He was a) removed from his polluting influence of the governor, and b) as he was led about by the hand, he was given a season to consider leaving his service to the prince of darkness, and instead serve the Light of the world.

The Spirits of Bala'am and Jezebel in the Early Church

In Revelation 2:14-16, the church at Pergamum is rebuked for people in their midst who held to the teaching of Bala'am, with the attendant idolatry and sexual immorality. In 2:18-25, the church at Thyatira is rebuked for tolerating "that woman Jezebel, who calls herself a prophetess." She was an adulteress who was leading people into sexual immorality and idolatry, and teaching "Satan's so-called deep secrets." In other words, sorcery within the church, which denudes any authority for the church to produce godly counsel at the right hand of power; sorcery with the same effect as what Bala'am and Jezebel did to Israel.

Light and Dark in St. Michael's Chapel

As I have pursued the power to live in the light, I never consciously sought out the darkness to war against, whether in ethical or spiritual terms, but I ran into it nonetheless.

In the spring of 1972, I had a most remarkable encounter, in the very chapel in prep school where the Lord had filled me with the light of his presence in November 1967. The chapel's name, interestingly, is St. Michael's, named after the warring angel who defeats Satan in Revelation 12:7-9.

I was up late one evening in the dining room of the Old Building doing some work when a friend burst in, horrified, on me and several other seniors. He described to us in halting breaths how he had been waiting in the chapel for another friend to finish some work in the adjacent library. As he waited, the communion bells rang out three times from the balcony. Thinking he was being spoofed by someone, he called out for the prankster to reveal himself. Silence. So he climbed the wooden stairs to the balcony, searched it, and saw that nobody was there. There was no place to hide apart from where he searched, no other stairs, and all footsteps in that small chapel were most audible. A sense of abiding and evil darkness overtook him, and he fled in horror down the hill to the Old Building.

I was the only one of the several seniors there who took him seriously (or was willing to admit it). But too, I recently learned that the friend he was waiting for had a similar experience some weeks earlier. He was in the chapel late one evening, keeping track of some under-formers in the adjacent building. Then the chapel bell rang three times, no one on the campus heard it, and a dark and foreboding sense of evil came in.

In my young faith, I believed there was nothing to fear, so I suggested that we return to the chapel and investigate. It was just past midnight, and as we came within 20 to 30 feet of the chapel, we both looked into the windows. What we saw was a darkness that was blacker than black against the diffused light of nearby buildings, pulsating, alive, extraordinarily evil and very angry at our presence. Another step and we stopped, having come against a terribly tangible but invisible wall of air that was thicker than thick, impenetrable and driving us back. All my critical faculties were alert, and the experience was as real as anything I have known with the five senses. My friend and I turned and fled. I prayed until 4:00 a.m., trying to understand it.

I do not yet fully understand exactly what I came across, but I have some clues. First, I now know that the "witching hour" is from midnight to 3:00 a.m., when covens of witches (and/or warlocks on occasion) regularly meet to do their rituals and to curse their enemies, especially Christians. They prefer certain days and seasons on their pagan calendars, related ultimately to astrological factors. The evil presence was gathering just before midnight when my friend was initially spoofed.

Second, there is significance to the topographical region of the nearby Berkshire Hills. In this region there is found a high concentration of neo-pagan and occultic centers, and uniquely tied into New York City money, in the midst of the "power alley" of the Boston to New York to Washington corridor. This corridor is the most influential section of elitism in the nation, with the academic capital of Boston, the media and financial capital of New York City, and the political capital of Washington, D.C. Its international influence is also unparalleled. "Sorcery at the right hand of power"?

And third, I wonder what specific relationship this demonic manifestation had in terms of the name of St. Michael's chapel, and any spiritual turf at stake in the heavenlies. As well, the graveyard behind the chapel is where the wife of the man reputed to be Jack the Ripper (whom she murdered in England) is buried; and there is a history of many "ghost" stories told over the years, perhaps serving as a haunt for demons.

I was blown away by this experience at the time. The very chapel where the supernatural presence of Yahweh descended on me in 1967 was the very chapel where this demonic presence bearing the mark of Satan himself assaulted my friend and me in 1972. The contest of the darkness seeking to displace the Light.

Witchcraft in the Midst of Massachusetts Politics

In 1988, as the head of a New England wide evangelical pro-life ministry, I conceived of and led a statewide non-binding public policy petition drive in Massachusetts: "In biological terms, when does an individual human life begin?" We provided four possible answers: a) conception, b) viability, c) birth, or d) a write-in option for voters to identify a different biological point. It was kept off the ballot by the Attorney General, a former board member of Planned Parenthood, and deeply opposed by Planned Parenthood, the Civil Liberties Union of Massachusetts and the Boston chapter of the National Organization for Women – working in conjunction. Our research showed that at least 80 percent of the voters were likely to say "conception." This would have been devastating to the abortion-rights movement – establishing an accurate definition of terms by means of informed choice, and upending the rationale of the 1973 U.S. Supreme Court *Roe* v. *Wade* decision legalizing human abortion. Had we done one simple legal step, we would have prevailed, but that is the nature of the devil, to find our weak points and exploit them.

We slowly gained a perspective that there was more than meets the eye – a wall of witchcraft behind the scenes. Beginning in June of 1989, we began a presence at New England's largest abortion center, Preterm, on Beacon Street in Brookline, adjacent to Boston. There were two other abortion centers on Beacon Street nearby, Repro and Planned Parenthood, and we were occasionally at Repro as well. In about two years worth of Saturdays, we saw 200 or more women walk away from their abortion appointments by their own choices, many to go to Crisis Pregnancy Centers, and some also found Christ. We had a presence in worship and conversation with abortion rights activists. Our signs had intelligent and non-accusatory questions that caused many people to do some real thinking. Our large banner said, "You have the power to choose life," and those seven words alone turned many women away from planned abortions.

We were consistently opposed by people, especially women, publicly cursing us in open allegiance to witchcraft. I happened once to converse with a woman in such a context who, upon learning that I had organized the statewide pro-life referendum, claimed that she and others in the Boston chapter of NOW had reviewed all our petitions and found many forgeries. Now it turns out that Boston NOW and others, had been contacted by someone within the government, moments after we turned in our signatures. The theme of sorcery at the right hand of power? In fact, we had the highest percentage of ratified signatures in state history according to one member of the Secretary of State's office. I asked the woman why, if there were so many forgeries, was there never even one challenge mounted against one signature? She did not answer.

One remarkable series of events marked this whole season. On August 9, I was up late one evening (just before midnight), finishing some work. I was usually in bed much earlier. I was sitting at the kitchen table, leaned back in my chair and went into prayer. As I did, I had a clear and strong vision.

In it I saw a room with crudely fastened bookshelves against a wall to the right. It was laden with books of an occultic nature, along with some cognate paraphernalia. Two windows with sheer curtains were to its left, straight ahead, overlooking a busy city street. I got the sense it was a second or third floor apartment in a neighborhood near Boston University.

At a table in front of the windows, four women were seated. My perspective had me gazing over the shoulders of three of them from the near corner of the table. There was one woman to my left at one end, next to a window to her left, with the right side of her profile discernable but not distinguishable. Two women were seated next to each other to my right, their backs toward me, facing the windows. I saw the face of the fourth woman, who was seated at the end of the table closest to the bookshelves. I recognized having seen her among the abortion-rights protestors at Preterm, led by the Boston chapter of NOW.

On the table was a crude straw figure with about 35 needles stuck into it. As I looked at the figure, the Lord spoke to me and said that the straw

99

figure had been designed to represent me, and that these women were trying to work voodoo curses against me. I also had the sense they were amateurs at voodoo, but trying hard nonetheless, opening themselves up to whatever spiritual powers were necessary to succeed in disarming our Christian pro-life witness at Preterm.

The Lord then told me: "Command the needles to explode outward." I was surprised by the word "explode," and immediately rejoined that I was sure the Lord did not intend for the "exploding" needles to hurt any of the women. Being thus assured, I then commanded the needles "to explode outward in the name of Jesus." As I did, I saw the needles pop out of the straw figure and fall onto the table – as the vision was an ongoing event like watching a live television report.

As the needles popped out, the four women fell back in their chairs, knowing that this was the power of the Lord at work through my prayers. In other words, they were somehow aware that I was praying at that exact moment, and that the power of the God of the Bible was manifest in response to my prayers. The falling back of the women was as if they were struck by a powerful blast of wind.

That was the end of the vision, and I sat there amazed and surprised, not knowing fully what to make of it, still processing the images that had been placed before my mind's eye. The vision was clear and real, but as always, I do not fully trust anything like this without testing it and seeing clear signs of confirmation. So I put it this vision on the "back burner" and went about my life and work.

Over the next week and a half, I found myself interrupted four or five times, at various times and places, with the Lord telling me to pray – for at that given moment one or several of these women, perhaps at times with others, were cursing me again. Usually a brief prayer was sufficient, but once while driving home in the middle of the day, I was impressed to pray for some twenty minutes.

On the evening of August 18, a Friday, I was preparing some new signs for the next morning's presence at Preterm. When I was done, I looked at my watch – exactly 12:01 a.m. Then, again, the same vision of August 9 returned, exactly the same in all details and outcome, and I understood that these four women were repeating the attempted voodoo curses again, at that very moment.

After I rebuked the curses in prayer, I was immediately flooded with a remarkable sense of God's presence and peace, went to bed and slept wonderfully. In my prior trips to Preterm I had slept poorly the prior nights, filled with anxieties and uncertainties. I needed to be up at 5:00 a.m., and instead of being exhausted, I awoke fully rested. God's Spirit had touched me after the final rebuke of the voodoo, and a victory had been won in this spiritual warfare with demonic powers.

The fruit was immediately evident. I had expected about 40 people from our Christian pro-life group to show up that Saturday, but we saw as many as 150 different supporters at some point between 7 a.m. and noon. Something had happened in the spiritual realms the night before. We had an average of 80 people at a given time, and the abortion-rights supporters were almost as many at a given time. Four or five people told me how "anointed" that morning was in terms of worship, sidewalk counseling with abortion-minded women, and our witness to the abortion-rights activists. That word "anointed" had never been used before or since at Preterm. At least seven women chose not to follow through with their abortion appointments, and only twenty or thirty women were observed going into Preterm that morning, compared with fifty or so on prior Saturdays. Our people found that the abortion-rights activists had an uncharacteristic openness in the many conversations that occurred, and as well, whereas in our prior times at Preterm we noted pubic displays of witchcraft against us, we saw none that morning.

This was perhaps my first experience in "warfare prayer," that is, praying for God to break demonic powers in the hearts and minds of people who would otherwise resist the Gospel, and instead experience a level playing field to truly consider it.

Demons at the University of New Hampshire

In the middle of this season, I participated in a debate over abortion at the University of New Hampshire (UNH) on October 2, 1989, with three advocates on both sides, with a packed auditorium of some 400 people.

After the debate, off to the side of the podium area, I sought out a Methodist minister who represented the Religious Coalition for Abortion Rights (RCAR), to follow-up with him on certain of the points we had debated. I had several students from Gordon-Conwell Theological Seminary with me, and along with perhaps a dozen others, we formed into a circle of discussion. Many students were still milling around or in the process of leaving, so there was a substantial din of background noise in the auditorium.

While speaking with the Methodist minister, I was interrupted by a woman who came in and stood to my left. She was an ardent pagan feminist, who had questioned me from the floor during the debate format itself. Her question had led to her public embarrassment because she had misunderstood something I said, which the rest of the audience clearly understood. Now she was loaded for bear.

In her intensity to try again to discredit me, she told me to "stop trying to force your religion on me." I was momentarily incredulous, for the power of informed choice had been the cornerstone of my comments that evening (as I will define in the next chapter). At that moment I was unprepared for such vehemence, so I merely responded at the ethical and intellectual level and said, "I am not forcing religion on anyone, only seeking to persuade people openly and honestly."

She gazed intently in response and declared, "Well, you know, my god is not your god!" At this point I gained the first glimmer that something other than intellectual or political debate was in view. A real spiritual chill, a temperature change, had been brought into the air, but before I had time to process what it meant. And without the time to process it, and being caught off guard, I sought to inject a little humor with understatement. I replied, "That's obvious." Then I continued, "Nonetheless, we both have freedom in a democratic society to try and persuade one another. You are free to try and persuade me, and I am free to try and persuade you."

Then, like an uncontrollable volcano rising from within her soul, in an unnaturally deep voice, she exclaimed, "Well, I don't believe in democracy!" In a normal discourse, I would have followed up and asked her if she were a Marxist, and I would have asked her to see if she embraced any form of informed choice.

But this was not a normal discourse. For as she spoke these words, a literal wind was released from her person, and it caused me and the other 15 or so people in the discussion circle to fall backward one or two feet, including the pagan woman herself. The Methodist minister looked at her with surprised disgust, turned away and left, and most everyone else also immediately turned away and left, in somewhat of a daze, thus ending the conversation. I did not know what to make of it, and as I drove back to Massachusetts that evening, I thought about little else.

The next day, I called the several seminary students who were there with me, to gauge their discernment. They all noted the same phenomenon, that of a wind being released from the woman's person and driving them back.

One student was Bill Wilder, now a Ph.D. in New Testament. He said that his momentary judgment was that he had thrown his hands up and fell back in a kind of automatic gesture of disbelief at her comment. But then he realized that those with him were also falling back simultaneously, and he knew he had not stepped back but was thrust back.

Bill also noted that as soon as the words and wind came out of her, it were as though it came out against her will, and that there was "something" in her trying to take the words back and mute the reality of the wind. It were as though an indiscrete manifestation had been made by a demon in reaction to the Gospel, and in a manifestation it would rather have not made so publicly.

I believe that this public display showed the true nature of the contest for the bystanders, discredited the abortion-rights argument, and thus served the reality of Satan's household being divided. The Methodist minister and others on the abortion-rights side of the issue wanted to distance themselves from her and this manifestation.

A demon had been squirming within her all night, at the proclamation of the Gospel in the context of the abortion debate, in hatred of the biblical power of informed choice. Suddenly I grasped how powerful the word of God is in the face of the devil, and at the phenomenological level. At UNH, I stepped on the tail of a demon, and then became markedly awakened to this reality.

Demonic Opposition to Ministry at Cornell University

After the debate at UNH, I relayed its experience in a Thanksgiving newsletter. While at Cornell University in January, I met with a husband and wife team in campus ministry, whom we will call Joe and Sue.

Sue was eager to speak with me. Once, in the fall of 1988, she was awakened at 3:00 a.m., being strangled at the throat by invisible hands or claws. She cried out in terror, asking Joe to pray for her. After a period of prayer, the strangulation receded and ceased. There were repeated attacks in the ensuing months, each time at exactly 3:00 a.m., as she was awakened by a cacophony of "noise," where "the whole room seemed alive and crawling with evil laughter, accusations, mockery." Sometimes the attacks ceased with a short period of prayer, but at least once, Joe and Sue had to pray until dawn.

This was new territory for them. A woman friend, who had experience as a third-world missionary, gave one piece of advice to Sue – namely, that when the demon showed up again, to command it to "name itself." So the next time it happened, Joe commanded the demon to name itself, and the whole room became still and quiet. Then Sue heard God's voice in the most direct way she had ever experienced. His word came to her, through her mind but originating outside it. He said to her, "Its name is 'the bold one.'" So she told this to Joe, and he said, "By the authority that the True Bold One, Jesus Christ, gives me, I command you to leave and not return."

As he did, Sue saw in her spirit the appearance of a "huge lumbering demon in the upper right corner of the room. It seems jillions of smaller demons shot out of the room and the big one went out, snarling and fuming." The peace of the Lord came over Joe and Sue and their home. They fell peacefully asleep and never again experienced this demonic attack. These 3:00 a.m. attacks – sorcery at the right hand of power in an academic setting?

Who Moved the Stones?

I ran into a remarkable series of events when we moved back to my native Connecticut in 1992. It began with a daytime vision.

I saw an image of a spearhead, superimposed on a map of Connecticut, running from northwest to southeast, from the Berkshires across the Massachusetts border, the width covering much territory including the capitol city of Hartford, and aiming toward New London on Long Island Sound. As I saw the vision, the Lord said one word: "Vacuum." That was it, and the vision departed.

Some weeks later, while driving on Route 8 just south of Winsted, I noticed an intricate pillar of stones in the wide median strip, atop a large boulder. It was two or three feet high and involved dozens of stones. Throughout the Bible we see such "sacred stones" used by pagans to mark spiritual territory – to dedicate their lands and buildings to a pagan deity. As well, we have examples such as Joshua 4, where the covenant community erected an altar of stones to commemorate an act of Yahweh Elohim in history.

Two days later, six of us were hiking on a nearby hill for the purpose of praying for revival in Connecticut, for justice and mercy in the name of Jesus to salt society. In one of my prayers, I asked the Lord if these were pagan stones in need of removal, due to their spiritual evil, and if so, would the Lord send his holy angels to tear them down?

Three days later, on June 21 (the summer solstice), they came down – with no human involvement to our knowledge. We later learned that they had been up for years. It became our conviction that these stones were marking the spiritual territory of the Berkshire Hills for pagan devotion, as I indicated their spiritual territory earlier. At this point where Route 8 changes from a divided to a single highway, it is where the topography clearly marks a "gateway" to the Berkshires. This pillar of stones was partially rebuilt several times, subsequently, but kept coming down, again, without any human involvement on our part. The last time I drove past that spot, in 2007, the large boulder was barren, with a bird sitting atop it, and a bush growing high on its northwest side. In the meantime I have heard reports of stones going up again.

In the fall of 1992 I concluded, in consultation with others, especially local pastors, that the vision of the spearhead represented the curses of Native Americans as they were unjustly expelled from the state in the 1700s and 1800s, through broken treaties, violence and gambling debts often attained through manipulated drunkenness. Earlier in the year, when my wife and I were visiting the Barkhamsted Reservoir, and in a time of prayer, we were overcome with a sense of the need for the White Man to repent of his sins against the Native Americans. As the final Natives worked their way up the Farmington River, through the Berkshires and finally out to Michigan through the agency of some Christian missionaries, they cursed the White Man's God and government. The spearhead vision covers the state capitol, and aims where the Mashantucket-Pequot reservation now stands – a huge center of casino gambling, where a small number of one-quarter to one-sixteenth blooded Indians now receive billions of dollars from gambling and related revenue. There followed the Mohegan reservation and its gambling center nearby. Injustice reversed in the human sense, yet the whole gambling industry is now shrinking and in real danger of collapse due to its intrinsic nature.

We believed too that the word "vacuum" reflected a) how a vacuum cleaner removes all but the most stubborn dirt, being that of Christian influence; and b) like the gravity of a black hole keeps light from escaping, so too the Christian missionary effort had been held back in this area by demonic gravity. Near the land covered by the spearhead is Northampton,

Massachusetts, where the First Great Awakening began in the 1730s, and within it is Enfield, Connecticut, where the Second Great Awakening began a century later. Since the late 1800s, the spiritual vitality of evangelical Christianity in New England has suffered greatly, to the point of being the least evangelical and most skeptical corner of the nation.

A Witch and a Modest Prayer Meeting

In the spring of 1993 I had opportunity to visit with a pastor in Groton, Connecticut. He told me about a remarkable visit he had recently by a witch who approached him after a worship service. She announced herself and said that in New London County there were three covens of witches assigned to curse every pastor who also resides there, and that there was at least one coven dedicated to curse every pastor statewide. She also said that the curses had three priorities: first that the pastor would fall into theological error; second, into financial ruin; and third, into sexual sin. She then left.

I found this amazing. Since when do witches come into the open and announce their agendas? Since the devil is described as a lion on the prowl by the apostle Peter, it would seem that those in the occult would only risk open terrain a) if they were utterly confident in easy pickings, or b) if they were desperate for a meal. Was this public confrontation a sign of increased pluck on the part of occultists, believing Connecticut was in their control? Or was it a sign that they sensed a rumble under the templates of the culture that God's Spirit was about to move, and this was an attempted bravado seeking to cover fear?

That June, I also started a modest series of "warfare prayer" meetings at St. James Episcopal Church in Winsted. This term, used by C. Peter Wagner in a book by the same title, refers to strategic demonic powers that seek to control cities and nations – just as Daniel encountered the "prince of Persia" and "prince of Greece" as cited earlier. We prayed concerning the specific dynamics of Connecticut's spiritual territory, choosing Winsted because of proximity to the former pillar of stones on Route 8.

We sensed that both realities were spiritually tied into the geography of those hills, and that as the curses of the spearhead were aimed from there at Hartford and down to New London County, we wanted to pray in the same direction, essentially for religious, political and economic blessings for all people in the state.

Slander, Stones and Intimidation by a Lawyer

Let's take the view of a secular skeptic for a moment. Can any of this be psychoanalyzed or reduced to mere coincidence?

What followed in the ensuing years was again remarkable. An activist with Planned Parenthood and the National Abortion Rights Action League (NARAL) started tracking me. She got on my mailing list (incognito), and began to feed slander to quite a number of newspapers in New York, Connecticut and Massachusetts.

In this season, in between truckloads while moving across town, someone erected a pillar of stones on a rock outcropping next to our new house. Checking in?

Then the woman who was tracking me attended a Mars Hill Forum I addressed. The next day at the University of Connecticut, she addressed a meeting called "Keeping an Eye on the Radical Right" (though I make no such identification, as one newspaper writer noted). A friend of mine happened to see the poster just beforehand, and dropped in moments before she said, "But watch out for John Rankin. He is the most dangerous man in the state, for two reasons. First, because is a Harvard graduate, and second, because he believes that through prayer he can kick the devil out of the state." She was fearful of true prayer in the power and name of Jesus.

Then in the midst of this I learned that a lawyer in Winsted was investigating our prayer meeting on the grounds that we might be plotting to "violate the civil rights" of people. And a newspaper reporter working in conjunction with the lawyer (I later discerned) interviewed me about our prayer meeting and asked specifically if we "pray against people." I said a clear no, yet at the end of the interview she said, "Now let me review some of the major points we covered, to be sure I understand you clearly. First, you are praying against people, right?"

The agenda was clear, so I challenged her, every reporter from these other newspapers, and the lawyer head-on. As a result, the slander stopped and never came up again.

When those stones came down in 1992, I believe that the occultic powers in Connecticut were shaken. The occultists knew their spiritual power had been muted, and as soon as they fingered me, the campaign to take me down began. Sorcery at the right hand of power?

This whole campaign of opposition and slander against me traces back to that event on June 21, 1992. If that matter, and related experiences I had in the context of spiritual warfare, could all be written off as happenstance, as naturally explainable coincidences, then these questions remain: Why such a persistent reaction to it? Why not just put the stones back up and expect them to remain, absent natural opposition that could be fingered? If prayer has no power, why go to the point of published slander and hiring an attorney to oppose a prayer meeting? And if the opposition were just political in nature, why would I be called "dangerous" because of my commitment to prayer and its opposition to the devil?

A Remarkable Demonic Assault

In February of 2005, while returning home one night from teaching at New York Divinity School, I was suddenly overwhelmed with a devastating physical exhaustion.

For the next six weeks I slept 12-14 hours a day, and was not able to be productive in my waking hours. As a result, my finances went from a healthy trajectory to a disaster, and our home eventually went into foreclosure, which we later escaped only by the skin of our teeth.

In this time period, I was working on the Ministers Affirmation on Marriage, a document where I recruited 700 ministers and church leaders in Connecticut as signatories: "Yes to Man and Woman in Marriage: No to Same-Sex Marriage." In its 2003 and 2005 publication in the Hartford Courant, no one in the state – media, same-sex marriage advocates, academics, politicians, activists, et al. – raised one public question about its content and nature. And Connecticut, per capita, is the most educated and wealthy in the nation, the most skeptical of biblical faith.

At the six-week mark, I had seriously been considering writing a will, and how to make provision for my family as life was ebbing away. One friend said I looked like "the walking dead." Then, one day at my desk, suddenly it hit me. This exhaustion was not physical in origin, but demonic. Why was I not aware of this? And especially, in face of the work I was then seeking to accomplish. So I created an email group of some 70 men, and asked them to intercede in prayer for my deliverance.

The next morning, when I awoke, the exhaustion was gone, my health and energy fully restored, and there has been no return of this exhaustion since. Sorcery at the right hand of power?

The Power to Live in the Light

The Bible is clear: Where light is fully present, darkness by definition will flee. In keeping with the power of the physics of light versus darkness are, so too we are called to pursue the ethical power to live in the light, and accordingly, we will have true power to see the Light trump the darkness in spiritual warfare. I have some modest experience in these matters, and nothing I have encountered in decades of following Jesus can hold a candle to the truth of the Gospel. The Gospel is good news, available to all who seek truth for its own sake.

◆ ◆ ◆

Chapter Three
The Power of Informed Choice

Of Prime Importance

The most important verb in the Bible is "to eat," at least when it comes to defining human nature. This metaphor is also the basis for the power of informed choice, namely the idea that freedom is "an unlimited menu of good choices" defined in Genesis 2. This menu is protected when we do not eat poison and die. All things being equal, the real question is: Who does not enjoy eating – sharing a good feast with family and friends? I have asked this of many churches, and when they agree, I turn to the pastor and say, "Your church is theologically unified." I have asked this of various pagan and secular audiences, and they too agree.

Or to take it from another angle, it is fun to speak to a college audience with many skeptics present, and announce my subject matter: "Tonight I will be addressing the subjects of food, drink and sex." Do you think the students are interested? I continue: "Food without gluttony, drink without drunkenness, and sex within marriage – one man, one woman, one lifetime." All true freedom has proper boundaries. Without such boundaries, licentiousness and chaos are the inevitable result, to the destruction of freedom.

Pagans at Yale

In November 1995, Margot Adler was my guest at a Mars Hill Forum at Yale University. Margot is a reporter for National Public Radio (NPR) and widely read practitioner of Wiccan religion (in her book *Drawing Down the*

Moon). She makes a direct challenge to the "Judeo-Christian" tradition as being exploitative and against human freedom in many ways, and celebrates instead a pagan definition of freedom – freedom from sin and guilt, "religion without the middleman." She also relays the Wiccan creed: "An ye harm none, do what ye will." Yet during and after the forum itself, Margot expressly thanked me for my definition of the biblical nature of human freedom, the power of informed choice.

Most poignant was the testimony of a woman student. She stood up in the audience and said my biblical definition of freedom was the most beautiful she had ever heard, and then publicly lamented how she had never heard it when growing up in the church. After the forum, she described to me how she worshiped "the goddess" and subscribed to a pantheistic "earth-based religion" that gave her a sense of tranquility in the midst of nature, among a circle of like-minded women friends. She then asked, "Have you ever preached this in churches? Do you speak to college students about this? You should."

Also in 1995, I was meeting at the headquarters of Dr. Paul Kurtz's secular humanist organization outside Buffalo. I joined Paul for a free-flowing conversation, along with Tim Madigan, then editor of *Free Inquiry*, and Dr. Gordon Stein, editor of the *Encyclopedia of Unbelief*. I had addressed prior Mars Hill Forums with both Paul and Gordon. In the conversation, Tim affirmed all the biblical ethics of which I spoke, then said, "But John, aren't you just a nice guy who is adding these ethics to the Bible to make it more palatable?" I assured him, that while I appreciate being called a nice guy, no, I was not adding them to the Bible – I was deriving them from the Bible on its own terms.

As I gave definition to the power of informed choice, rooted in Genesis 2, Gordon then challenged me. "John," he said, "I am sure I can find scholars at Harvard or elsewhere who will disagree with your definition of freedom in Genesis." I answered, "Gordon, you can find many scholars at Harvard or elsewhere who will disagree with the trust I place in the Bible as God's inspired Word. But you cannot find one scholar who can give evidence that I have misrepresented what Genesis 2 says on its own terms, about how it defines freedom." Gordon was an avowed atheist, but he loved this definition of freedom.

The Golden Rule

In the field of comparative religions, it is often noted that most world religions have some expression of the Golden Rule. But do they?

The Golden Rule is taken from Jesus' words in the Sermon on the Mount:

> "So in everything, do to others what you would have them do to you, for this sums up the Law and the Prophets" (Matthew 7:12).

Jesus also framed the Golden Rule during Passion Week:

> " 'Love the Lord your God with all your heart and with all your soul and with all your mind [and with all your strength].' This is the first and greatest commandment. And the second is like it: 'Love your neighbor as yourself.' All the Law and the Prophets hang on these two commandments" (Matthew 22:37-40; brackets from [Mark 12:30]; cf. Luke 10:27).

We are to give to others as God has given to us, as the apostle John reiterates in his first epistle when he says that we love because God first loved us (1 John 4:19). And we are to live out the Golden Rule in tangible reality, as Jesus taught in the Parable of the Good Samaritan (Luke 10:25-37), where he defined the neighbor whom we are to love – even our enemy. In other words, the Golden Rule is based on the power to give, and it equals the centrality of the Law of Moses that Jesus came to fulfill.

But note how it is expressed positively: we love God as he loves us, thus we are to initiate the act of giving to others. "Do to others ..." Or we can translate it, "Treat others as you would have them treat you."

In contrast, other religions frame it negatively: Do not do to others what you do not want them to do to you. This is known as the "silver rule," where a reactive negation of the negative is the highest view of how to pursue the positive. It is rooted in a position of an original freedom not given or known. In Hinduism it is: "This is the sum of duty: Do nothing unto others which would cause pain if done to you." In Confucianism it is: "Is there one word that will keep us on the path to the end of our days? Yes, Reciprocity. What you do not wish yourself, do not unto others." In Buddhism it is: "Do not harm, but stop harm." Even a post-biblical Judaism falls into a negative construct: "What is hateful to you, do not to your fellow man. That is the entire law; all the rest is commentary." (Too, has a post-biblical Christianity fallen prey to the same?) Islam is claimed as an exception to this, where it states: "None of you has faith unless he loves for his brother what he loves for himself." The problem here is that "his brother" has historically been understood to refer uniquely or principally to a fellow Muslim, not an outsider, especially an "infidel." And as we saw above in Margot Adler's Wiccan ethic, which is historically much more recent, "An ye harm none, do what ye will."

Thus, the highest concept of freedom outside of biblical foundations is negative – freedom from violation. This ethic says that if you do not violate others, they will (hopefully) not violate you. This is admirable, for who wants to be violated? We all seek salvation from violation. But is it a salvation from, or a salvation to? Without the proactive definition of human freedom found in the biblical order of creation, the highest hope is a negative one. Or as the pathos of Janis Joplin's 1970 dirge in *Me and Bobby McGee* puts it: "Freedom is just another word for nothing left to lose, Nothing, that's all Bobby left me..." A negative freedom satisfies no one ultimately.

The First Words in Human History

In chapter 1, we noted the first words in history, when God created the universe and said, "Let there be light." These words reflect God's sovereign power, and that power is the power to give, leading to the power to live in the light, all of which reflects his freedom to do the good. Therefore, on the Bible's own terms, the sovereignty of God's nature is the starting point for all true doctrine, and the root for our human story.

There is nothing that precedes God's sovereignty, for apart from his sovereignty nothing else could exist. This means that the sovereign God provides human freedom, and the relationship between God's sovereignty and our freedom is the most important relationship in all Scripture and life.

Thus, sovereignty equals the biblical starting point for describing God's nature, and freedom equals the biblical starting point for describing human nature.

The text of Genesis 2:16-17 gives us the first recorded words of Yahweh to man:

And the LORD God commanded the man, "You are free to eat from any tree in the garden; but you must not eat from the tree of the knowledge of good and evil, for when you eat of it you will surely die."

These are the words of human freedom, the power of informed choice. Freedom begins with a command that is also a statement of fact: "You are free..." Or in other words, the language of Yahweh's commandments is the language of freedom. It begins with the sovereign God whose will, from the beginning, is for us to be free.

An Unlimited Menu of Good Choices

This command, "You are free to eat," can be better grasped by knowing the power of the Hebrew idiom in use. The Hebrew words *akol tokel*, are robustly translated, "In feasting you will continually feast." The grammatical idea is like an active particle, with the sequential use of the infinitive and imperfect tenses for "eat," a feast that never stops feasting. It is the idea of an unlimited menu of good choices – not only in terms of food options in the Garden of Eden, but also in the application of this metaphor to all moral and aesthetic choices in life.

This language of eating and feasting, with implicit drink, defines the rest of the Bible. Old Testament worship revolves around the feasts of Passover, Unleavened Bread, Firstfruits, Pentecost, the Day of Atonement (*yom kippur*), Tabernacles, Sacred Assembly and Purim. Isaiah, in a messianic prophecy, gave the invitation to come, eat and drink without cost. Jesus celebrated the wedding supper at Cana, gave the invitation to the wedding supper of the Lamb, prophesied that he would again drink wine in the kingdom of heaven, instituted the Eucharist or Lord's Supper, ate fish as proof of his resurrection body, and the Holy Spirit beckons us to the wedding supper of the Lamb in Revelation as well. The final act of redemption, in the last chapter of Revelation, is the provision for the river of the water of life (22:1) and the tree of life (22:2). In Jesus' final words, he invites us to partake of the tree of life (22:14), and after the Spirit gives his final invitation of "Come!" (to the banquet), the apostle John adds, "Whoever is thirsty let him come; and whoever wishes, let him take the free gift of the water of life" (22:17).

Feasting permeates Scripture from beginning to end; it is the metaphor of human freedom (*akol tokel*). This is the freedom to feast from an unlimited menu of good choices – to satisfy our eagerness, hunger and thirst for life (the deepest significance of *nephesh*). Or to sum it up theologically: "Taste and see that the LORD is good" (Psalm 34:8).

But access to this feast requires a moral understanding of the freedom to choose between good and evil, and the feast of Genesis 2:16 carried with it the caveat, boundaries and structures for the power of informed choice. All humanity knows protective boundaries in daily life, from gravity to a highway median strip to a thousand other examples.

In Genesis 2:17 we see the "but." The unlimited menu of good choices had a restriction that is in reality a boundary of protection. Namely, freedom cannot exist without boundaries. Thus, Yahweh defined the power of informed choice. The protection of an unlimited menu of good choices requires the prohibition of a singular evil choice:

> "But you must not eat from the tree of the knowledge of good and
> evil, for when you eat of it you will surely die."

To understand the trees of Genesis 2:15-17, we must return to Genesis 2:9:

> And the LORD God made all kinds of trees grow out of the
> ground—trees that were pleasing to the eye and good for food. In the
> middle of the garden were the tree of life and the tree of the
> knowledge of good and evil.

This phrase, "the knowledge of good and evil," referred to Adam's given authority on the one hand, and possibly the use of a Hebrew idiom, on the other. Adam and Eve were created to rule over the creation, under God, and thus in accordance with his definitions of good and evil. To eat of the forbidden fruit was for man and woman to say a) God is not good, that he must be withholding something good from us in the prohibition, that is to say, calling God evil; b) thus, to rationalize the will to disobey God; c) to redefine good and evil; and d) thus, to lift ourselves up to the level of God, if not actually seeking to transcend him.

119

To challenge God's goodness is the basic nature of unbelief. In the letter to the Hebrews, the writer speaks of faith as the quality of believing that God rewards those who earnestly seek him (see 11:1-6). God is good and worthy of invested faith.

Being limited within the good boundaries of time, space and number, how can we think we can redefine God's terms and realities, and live in his universe? To eat the forbidden fruit was to redefine good and evil over and against God. Instead, man was to judge good and evil in the universe congruent with God's definition of terms, recognizing the forbidden fruit as a test and a boundary.

Another factor is a Hebrew idiom for that which is comprehensive. Namely, the polar opposites of "good and evil" can refer literally to the knowledge of everything. Everything there is to know lies in the spectrum between good and evil. The polar opposites of beginning and end are likewise comprehensive in defining time (see Isaiah 44:6; 48:12; Revelation 1:8; 21:6; 22:16). The polar opposites of height and depth, of east and west, are likewise comprehensive in defining space (Psalm 103:11-12).

Therefore, "the knowledge of good and evil" here is a concept that equals a whole unit. It is knowledge that only God as the uncreated Creator can possess. As well, only God can know the totality of intrinsic evil without being tempted or polluted by it. Evil is ethically the absence of God's presence, the absence of true ethics, which means the absence of true relationships. To know good and evil is to define it, in the sense of this Hebrew idiom – something only God can do. Adam and Eve were called to judge between good and evil, but based on God's true definitions. People who seek to define good and evil differently than God does, have become their own gods

Accordingly, as a creature made in God's image, there was nothing "good" withheld from Adam, as the *akol tokel* idiom of positive freedom already established. He had been given the "tree of life" to eat from, a tree which is the source for eternal life. Metabolically, it must have contributed to the eternal renewal of all the cells in our bodies. Alongside that tree is the forbidden fruit – forbidden if we wish to live. Metabolically, it must have assaulted the renewal of our bodily cells. Then morally, relationally, to eat of the tree of the knowledge of good and evil equals an attempt to digest what we cannot, as if we who are limited by space, time and number, can grasp or wrap ourselves around eternity. We will explode first.

The choice between good and evil is powerfully portrayed by a parallelism in vv. 16 and 17. The phrase "you will surely die" is likewise better grasped by the power of the idiom in place. The Hebrew here reads *moth tamuth*, which literally means, "in dying you will continually die." It is the exact parallel of *akol tokel* in terms of grammatical construct (but with opposite moral nature), with the sequential use of the infinitive and imperfect tenses for "die," carrying with it the force of an active participle – always dying, yet to die.

Thus, if we partake in the eternal quality of death, which the forbidden fruit introduces, we will continually experience the taste of death. This is the biblical root for the language and metaphors of hell – a chosen death that never stops dying. What this also means is that the definition of death is principally theological in nature, and not just in reference to the physical termination of life. Theological death is the brokenness of relationship with God and one another. It is alienation from Yahweh's presence. Adam thus "died," only to continue "dying." Adam and Eve had been given the tree of life to eat from continually, so as to live forever. Once they partook of the fruit of death, this alienation from God's full presence removed from their bodies the regenerative qualities of the tree of life, so they began to die.

Adam's physical life span was shortened from forever to 930 years, and the increase in sin's impact upon the body over the subsequent millennia has brought the average life span to well under 100 years.

This contrast of choices in Genesis 2:16-17 is marked, and the reader who knows the Hebrew would pick it up immediately:

in feasting you will continually feast, or

in dying you will continually die.

Another way of putting it is:

an unlimited menu of good choices, or

a limited menu of only death.

With parallel idioms in place, signaling opposite choices, the power of informed choice is defined:

feast or die.

The command to feast was God's will, but the warning against dying carried with it a power to disobey that will. The very language of "will," or "willpower," connotes the exercise of choice. God's choice is that we live forever, but he does not force it on us.

The Origin of Evil

But why would a loving God permit evil to happen? Outside the biblical worldview, the best attempts to understand the origin of evil are to assume it has always been there, in a dualistic tension and codependency with the good. And therefore the highest aspirations of dualistic religions can rarely see past a negative view of freedom – freedom from violation – which ultimately is an escape from suffering into the "nothingness" of a Hindu eternal destiny or similar concept.

This negative view of freedom was the highest concept of freedom imaginable to cultures that knew nothing of creation, sin and redemption. And it is in knowing these biblical doctrines that we find the key to knowing the origin of evil, for evil is a reversal of the order of creation. The simplicity of evil's origin may appear to some as a scandal; namely, the origin of evil lies in the goodness of God. (This is an ethical statement, prior to the concern about Satan's appearance, his nature and origin.) Evil is a parasite, just as darkness is to light.

Therefore, true goodness involves the permission to choose evil, with the power of informed choice being made available by God. Evil does not allow the permission to choose the good.

Evil is a choice, and God's goodness necessarily allows this choice because goodness is not forced. God's perfect will, and his loving, giving and good nature, is never diminished by this freedom that is given. The power of informed choice stands above reproach in every measure, and any human attempt to equal or surpass this definition of justice only adds further suffering. *Akol tokel* or *moth tamuth*. Feast or die – the choice is ours as the gift of the good and sovereign God.

Is this a scandal to say that the origin of evil comes as a direct result of the goodness of God? Only to those who have compromised the sovereignty and goodness of God.

Hell as an Object of God's Love

Another way of putting this is by interpolating the love of God in John 3:16 into the text of Genesis 2:16. In doing so, we come up with the following verse in the RSSV (the "Rankin Sub-Standard Version"):

> For God so loved the world, that he gave each one of us the freedom to go to hell, if that is damn well what we want to do.

Now, I use the word "damn" with theological precision – a curse people choose.

Only God can get away with giving this radical human freedom. Only God loves us enough to let us choose whether or not to accept his love. This is God's nature, the nature of the power to give, which uniquely provides a level playing field to choose between good and evil.

The nature of Satan is the power to take and destroy, and therefore, he is in no frame of mind to give us freedom to say no to evil, he has no interest in a level playing field. No pagan religion or secular construct allows a level playing field where good and evil are honestly defined and presented side by side, for they have no definitions of an original goodness. Thus the best they can offer is a hope to overcome evil and distrust, but without any means. Thus there is no informed choice, only one unhappy non-option.

God does not force his love on us, for that would deny his very goodness. Goodness is the power to give, and to be forced into accepting God's love is an oxymoron. Love is a gift, and human nature is predicated on the power to give. To be forced to do good would be evil. Or to be more graphic, forced love equals rape. For God to force his love on us would be evil, it would be pagan – it would be the surrender of his sovereignty, it would be a dualistic condescension to the devil's ethics. Here is the sequence:

Goodness equals the power to give;

Evil equals the power to take; thus

Goodness cannot be forced – it can only be a gift received by
informed choice.

Thus, goodness can never be forced, and when it is attempted, the good that was envisioned turns into evil. By the same token, evil can never act like a gift – it is always something that is deceptive and/or impositional. Another way of putting it is to say that, in the final analysis, love is a choice that cannot be faked, and hatred is a choice than cannot be hidden.

The nature of human freedom comes from God's nature. God is free, and as image-bearers of God, we are made to be free. But what is freedom? It is the power to do the good. Is God free to do evil? No. To do evil is to be a slave to it, and God is a slave to no thing. And the Creator, if infected by any destruction, could not sustain the universe. To do the good is to be free. But since we are finite, we must make the choice between good and evil, with both realities possible.

As image-bearers of God, if we were forced to accept God's will, the qualities of responsibility ("ability to respond") and creativity would be moot – we would be no more than animals or puppets. Love as a gift calls us to respond, and response involves the exercise of choice. Yahweh has taken the cosmic risk, that for the sake of those who choose "yes" to his love, there will be those who choose "no." The giving of love always involves risk in this sense of the word – the risk that our desire for others to receive our love might be rejected. In 1 Timothy 2:4, Paul says God desires all people to be saved, and in 2 Peter 3:9, Peter says that God wants nobody to perish, yet Scripture also says that not all people will be saved. The dynamics of freedom.

What therefore is God's perfect will? Simply, I understand that God's will, consistent with his nature in the power to give, is to give us the opportunity to choose whether or not to accept his will.

One way of illustrating this is to say that hell is an object of God's love. Those who choose hell are those who actually accept God's loving provision not to have his love shoved down their throats. When the Jewish context of Jesus' language of hell is examined, we see that those who choose hell are uniquely a (limited) class of people who enjoy causing injury to others. They are those who hate mercy for themselves (out of their pride) and mercy for others (out of an impositional attitude that is rooted in their pride).

I think of its moral nature in these terms. Most of us as adults know the reality of anger and bitterness. Bitterness is rooted in "trust betrayed," and if it is allowed to grow, it deadens the human spirit toward love and friendship. If this downward cycle of sin's vortex is not arrested and reversed through repentance and forgiveness, then the human soul becomes more perversely self-justified in its anger and bitterness. Ultimately, this bitterness is expressed toward God. People with such a hardened attitude toward God would rather stew in their juices than become humble in his presence. They (perversely) enjoy bitterness more than humility. We all know of people who would rather die in bitterness, than forgive someone who has betrayed them.

Though betrayed, to hold onto revenge is to play God, and to be destroyed by the *moth tamuth* of such folly, disobedience and lack of trust. The Bible says that vengeance is God's alone – he will repay (see Deuteronomy 32:35; cf. Romans 12:19). He alone has the mercy and righteousness to judge all men and women fairly. And he alone has the power to forgive for those who choose mercy over judgment. Those who enjoy revenge will be given its eternal and perverse enjoyment of its unending implosion. The redeemed will forsake revenge forever. It is a question of which we yearn for – mercy that triumphs over judgment, or self-righteous judgment that trumps mercy (see James 2:12-13).

There are two ways of accomplishing revenge against someone: the "pagan way" and the so-called "sanctified way." The pagan method is simply to push the person in front of an oncoming Mack truck. The "sanctified" method is to pray that the person will trip and fall into the path of an oncoming Mack truck. When the disciples wanted to call fire from heaven upon a Samaritan village that would not welcome Jesus, he rebuked them – no "sanctified" human revenge was allowed (Luke 9:51-56).

Vengeance belongs only to God, for he alone is sovereign, and completely just and fair, consistent with the power of informed choice.

Hell is that dark and therefore colorless community (which is really no community) of people who are satisfied in the fire of hate, in unforgiveness, self-righteousness, in bitterness and in moral darkness. They have forsaken the power to give, the power to live in the light, and the power to forgive. It is that domain where music cannot exist, for the very nature of music is predicated on order and harmony, whereas human irreconcilability equals the cacophony of discordant, sharp and abusive angles.

The writer of the letter to the Hebrews (see 6:4-8), and the apostle Peter (see 2:2:17-22), both address this reality as they speak of those leaders who by their own choice moved past the realm of forgiveness. The metaphor used by Jeremiah for the potter and the clay is also applicable (see 18:1-12). If we remain in the Potter's hands, we remain moist and moldable. If we excuse ourselves from the Potter's presence and influence, avoiding altogether or cutting short his work, we harden and crack. The more hardened we become, the more softening up we need for restoration. C.S. Lewis describes this in *The Great Divorce* as people who continually move away from each other, because they cannot stand friendship and the mutual trust and vulnerability it requires. There can come a point when a person becomes so far removed from God's presence that he sears his conscience.

On Judgment Day, those who have "longed for his appearing" (2 Timothy 4:8), who have come to Jesus on his own good terms (see Matthew 11:28-30), will rejoice as they are received into God's kingdom. *Akol tokel.* Those who have not loved God will detest his presence and wish to flee from it. They will get what and whom they have loved. *Moth tamuth.* In John 3:16-21 we saw how Jesus talked of those who loved darkness more than light because they knew their deeds were evil. Jesus came not to condemn but to save, so those who are condemned are self-condemned.

God's love is to give us what and whom we have chosen to love. Evil people will go to hell shaking their fists in defiance of God in the ultimate perversion of holding onto a self-righteousness that loves sin and pride more than truth and reality. They will love such a defiant stand, for the true heaven would be hell to them, and hell is their actual heaven. The moral dimensions of hell are remarkable, extraordinarily just, and understood as the necessary risk of God's love as evidenced in the power of informed choice.

"Theological Baggage"

This theology concerning the nature of hell is important, for the most common objection to the Gospel in our culture is "don't shove it down my throat." How often are people able to misinterpret the Gospel because they have not heard about the good order of creation, and the power of informed choice? Namely, they have encountered preaching that up front seeks literally "to scare the hell out of them." That is, if we start with the condemnation of hell, absent its moral dimensions of informed choice, we pollute the good news and it is seen as bad news. The good order of creation must be first defined – so the depths of sin can be understood in contrast, not as a starting point – and then the height of redemption can be grasped. An opposite error is to speak only of the goodness of redemption without rooting it in the order of creation and reality of the fall.

In 1991 I was invited to address a group known as the Democratic and Secular Humanists (DASH) meeting at the Phillips Brooks House at Harvard. The leader introduced me as "an evangelical minister who likes to be raked over the coals by skeptics." As part of my presentation I argued that any expression of order in the universe must come from a greater

Order, and that there is no evidence in all of human knowledge for a lesser order producing a greater order – for nothing producing something.

So I asked what came before the beginning of the universe. One man said "Eternal matter." I responded, "What then, in intellectual terms alone, is the difference between believing in eternal matter on the one hand, and an eternal God on the other? In both cases, we are accepting something greater than space, time and number, and something beyond our finite capacity to grasp."

He paused, then said, "Theological baggage."

As we unpacked these two words, it was clear he did not want to admit the possibility of a personal God. He feared that "believers" would then take the license to "shove religion down his throat." In other words, his resistance to the Gospel was at the ethical level – "do not violate my person" – not at the intellectual level. The true definitions of terms concerning heaven and hell need to be known; and as well, concerning the biblical power of informed choice versus the pagan and secular ethos that allows coercion.

Undeniable Justice

The justice of these ethics is profiled in Ezekiel 23, as rooted in the prior reality of Ezekiel 16, where the prophet ministered to the Hebrew exiles in Babylon in 593ff B.C. In a parable of two adulterous sisters, representing Samaria and Jerusalem, Ezekiel portrayed their lustings after the Assyrians and their idols, instead of loving Yahweh. Then v. 9 jumps out of the text: "Therefore I handed her over to her lovers, the Assyrians, for whom she lusted."

In other words, God hands us over to what and whom we have loved. What could be more just? God does not force us into heaven or hell. The text continues in v. 10:

> "They stripped her naked, took away her sons and daughters and killed her with the sword. She became a byword among women, and punishment was inflicted on her."

Choices have consequences. We reap what we sow, we can choose idols if we please, but God warns us of the consequences.

Those who deliberately reject the Savior will have an eternity of stewing in their juices, continually reaffirming their choices, growing more alienated, more lonely, in greater darkness and the gnashing of their teeth in self-righteousness, yet with a fire raging in their breasts – but never for an inch desiring the humility of reconciliation. They will increasingly want to slam their fists into the face of God, also into the face of one of his image-bearers, being aligned forever with the choice of the power to destroy. In this sense, heaven would be hell for the unbeliever, as hell is their chosen heaven.

We are not free to say yes to God, unless we are first free to say no. There is no commission in the Gospel to force, coerce, trick or deceive anyone into the faith. Those are the devil's ethics. If we honor the power to give and power of informed choice for all people equally, then those who say no to it will actually be receiving a gift, and thus confirming God's sovereign nature. They cannot then accuse God or his ambassadors of "shoving" it down their throats.

Those who hate God may shake their fists at him, but inside their souls they know they have no just cause for doing so. If there are those who receive this same freedom, and say no to the gift of saying no, which means saying yes, then the angels will rejoice (see Luke 15:7,10). In all capacities, we as servants of the Gospel will always be in the position of giving to others with no strings attached, based in the security of knowing God is sovereign and he alone judges the human heart. Accordingly, hell is an object of God's love, and those who choose residence in hell are still loved by God, in that he loved them enough to give them such a choice.

True and False Definitions of Terms

In Genesis 2:9, the text defines the two trees in the middle of the Garden – one leads to eternal life and the other leads to eternal death. Yahweh therefore lays the basis for Adam and Eve to make their choice. This sets up a contrast of opposing ethical systems:

God's ethics = true definition of terms = informed choice
= life;
Satan's ethics = false definition of terms = misinformed
choice = death.

There are good ethics, and there are evil ethics. Telling the truth, indeed, "truth in advertising," is the same as the power to live in the light, and it is the means for discerning the difference.

In Genesis 2:17, God told Adam that if he disobeyed and ate of the forbidden fruit, then *moth tamuth*, "in dying you will continually die." In Genesis 3:1-5, we see how Satan, incarnate as the serpent, reversed the order of creation with false definition of terms, which led to misinformed choice, which led to death. In v. 4, the serpent said *lo muth tamuthon*, "In dying you will not continually die."

We can note how Satan's false definition of terms led to misinformed choice and therefore to death; in contrast to God's true definition of terms which leads to the power of informed choice, and therefore to life. When God said there is a tree of life, and a tree of death, he spoke accurately. On this basis, people can choose life.

The Testimony of Moses, Joshua and Elijah

The gift of human freedom, the power of informed choice and, therefore, its interpretive importance in defining human nature, is strategically restated as the Bible unfolds. We have it first in the words of God to Adam, then restated in the final public words of Moses, the final public words of Joshua and, then in the shortest sermon in the Bible, delivered by Elijah in the apex of prophetic witness against Israel's apostasy.

Moses

In Deuteronomy 30:11-20, Moses brought to a conclusion his long sermon, the final public words of his life before the Israelites entered the Promised Land. He declared the accessibility of the power of informed choice, setting before us "life and prosperity, death and destruction" (v. 15). This is the exact choice given Adam and Eve in the Garden, even now in the face of human sin – *akol tokel* or *moth tamuth*.

We do have the power to choose life, for Moses says, "Now choose life" (v. 19). But to have such power does not mean our sinful nature has the ability to achieve salvation, to "ascend into heaven" as it were; rather, that there is within our fallen humanity the remains of God's image sufficient enough to say "help," and whether we say "help" is a matter of the human will.

Our human spirit as touched by the Holy Spirit can respond to God. In fact, this power of informed choice was fully in place for Cain before he murdered Abel, one generation after the exile of his parents from the Garden of Eden. He could have mastered the sin "crouching at (his) door," but instead he chose to let it come in and master him (Genesis 4:6-7). The Hebrew verb at play refers to a leopard prepared to spring on its prey, yet man and women were originally given authority over the animal kingdom. Cain chose to be mastered.

Joshua

When Israel completed its conquest of Canaan, as much as they would, Joshua gave his final public address at Shechem. In Joshua 24:14-24, he reiterated the goodness of Yahweh through the Exodus, so that all Israelites had the basis for informed choice. This covenant on the plains of Shechem was the final gathering of the exodus community, and Joshua sent them off with a passionate appeal. He used a powerful form of dissuasion, requiring the Israelites to count the cost of discipleship before they said yes. Joshua was pressing them toward the freedom to choose "no" in order to ensure the integrity of their "yes." No games, no manipulations, no trickery. Joshua was basing his appeal on God's ethics of true definition of terms.

Theocracy as a Community of Choice

In verse 15 Joshua's language is remarkable:
> "But if serving the LORD seems undesirable to you, then choose
> for yourselves this day whom you will serve, whether the gods your
> forefathers served beyond the River, or the gods of the Amorites, in
> whose land you are living. But as for me and my household, we will
> serve the LORD."

The term "undesirable" comes from the Hebrew root of *ra*, which most simply means "evil." Joshua was inviting them to serve other religions if they found anything evil, anything less than desirable or reasonable in the requirements of the Law of Moses. Another way of looking at this is the fact that theocratic Israel was a "community of choice." God commanded blessings for those who would obey. His theocratic rule was not a forcing of unwanted legislation down their throats. Rather, God told them the exact boundaries of freedom, the power of informed choice. If they did not like or agree with such ethics, they were free to go to Babylonia, Egypt, among the Canaanites, specifically here the Amorite tribe, or elsewhere.

They were free to leave anytime if they thought anything Yahweh said or did was evil. But if they chose to stay in theocratic Israel, it was because they knew and trusted the goodness, justice and provisions of Yahweh Elohim, as demonstrated by the signs and wonders of the Exodus. Yahweh had earned their trust. They knew Yahweh's goodness. They were free to choose to become part of the "chosen people."

Never in the Law of Moses are Yahweh's laws forced on pagans, nor should his goodness be forced on skeptics. This would be an oxymoron. The Gospel is the good news of winning people's choice to love God as he has loved them.

There is also an interesting balance between the words of Moses and Joshua. Moses emphasized the accessibility of making the right choice, and Joshua emphasized its difficulty. This is part of the *merismus* of Scripture, "a little part here, a little part there" – when different elements are emphasized in different contexts, in a cooperative tension in the balance of the whole, in the very nature of a storyline. This reflects the balance between God's sovereignty and human choice. The right choice is accessible if we accept God's grace and admit our needs in his sight; it is inaccessible if we depend on the sinful nature. Joshua was pressing the Israelites hard to discern the difference.

Elijah

When Israel was led by Ahab and Jezebel, the prophet Elijah challenged the 450 prophets of Ba'al and the 400 prophetesses of Asherah to a contest on Mount Carmel (see 1 Kings 18:16-40). The devotees of Ba'al called on their god to answer with fire from heaven, but in spite of daylong prayer and self-flagellation, there was no response. But Yahweh answered Elijah the moment he prayed. In his public address to the apostate Israelites beforehand, Elijah was succinct in assuming the power of informed choice:

> "How long will you waver between two opinions? If the LORD is God, follow him; but if Baal is God, follow him."

> But the people said nothing (v. 21).

The power of informed choice, as defined at these interpretively key junctures, continues through the balance of Scripture. Jeremiah said to Israel that if they wanted to go ahead and sin, then they were free to do so (see 15:1-2). He knew they knew the power of informed choice, and that they had chosen disobedience. The power of informed choice is the invitation to believe, given in the gospels (see Matthew 11:28-30), all the way to the final invitation in the book of Revelation (see 22:17).

Sovereignty and Choice

The balance between God's sovereignty and human choice has occasioned much debate in church history, and is a huge subject. For here, consistent with the biblical power of informed choice, we can make some observations. Again, we start with the observation that the first words in Scripture underscore God's sovereign power: "In the beginning God created..." And God's first words in human history underscore human freedom: "You are free to eat..." The sovereignty of God provides for the freedom of man.

There is a necessary and positive tension between sovereignty and choice, like a spring or coil calibrated to the exact tension needed to perform its task of maintaining the proper balance and integrity of a larger mechanism. Or like the tension between electrons and protons surrounding the neutrons, necessary for the integrity of molecular structure and the existence of the universe. Such tensions produce the freedom for man and woman to live and prosper. It produces the balance between worship and responsibility.

Jars of Clay

This tension and balance can be easily seen in 2 Corinthians 4:7:

> But we have this treasure in jars of clay to show that this all-surpassing power is from God and not from us.

Another way of translating "jars of clay" is by "cracked pots," that is, leaky vessels. We are called to acknowledge that we are cracked pots, and therefore not crackpots. By confessing our humanity and fallibility we embrace reality, whereas a crackpot flees reality. The reality is that we have this "treasure" of God – the gift of his Holy Spirit who seals the promised eternal life – in our human frame, to demonstrate God's power.

And what is God's power? He is so totally in control, that he can place his perfect gift in imperfect vessels, and achieve a perfect result (in the Hebrew, not Platonic sense). His sovereignty is not wooden, so that it has to condescend to manipulating the human will within the confines of space, time and number.

Rather, his sovereignty is so great, that he alone can afford to give genuine human freedom, and not be diminished in the process, because he is sovereign. If God were diminished by the act of giving human freedom, then he would not be free to begin with – having been reduced to a pagan deity. Pagan deities are limited creatures (literally demons), and they diminish their pretense if they attempt an act of giving. Giving and pretense cannot coexist peacefully.

No Judgment Apart from Chosen Deeds

Nowhere in Scripture are people judged by God apart from the consequences of their chosen deeds. They are never judged for deeds they did not do, or did not choose to do. This language is found often, where the tension and balance between sovereignty and choice is obvious.

We reap what we sow. Hell is that oxymoronic community of choice, populated by people who consciously choose no to God – whether no to his covenant revelation, or no to the revelation Paul speaks about in Romans 1-2. Heaven is that true community of choice, populated by people who choose yes to God and therefore to the completed work of Jesus Christ – whether yes to his covenant revelation, or yes to the revelation Paul speaks about in Romans 1-2.

What About Those Who Have Never Heard?

In Romans 1, Paul begins his concerns with the order of creation, and how godlessness among all people will be judged, for all people "knew God." In Romans 2, Paul works with tightly constructed language emphasizing the inseparability of belief and action, saying:

> God "will give to each person according to what he has done." To those who by persistence in doing good seek glory, honor and immortality, he will give eternal life. But for those who are self-

137

seeking and who reject the truth and follow evil, there will be wrath and anger (vv. 6-7).

Everything Paul asserts in Romans 1-2 is consistent with the image of God in the order of creation, and with the power of informed choice. Without distinguishing between Jew and Gentile, he says that we will gain what we seek – eternal life for those who do good, and wrath for those who are self-seeking.

Then Paul speaks about how those who sin will be judged by the law they know – either covenant revelation for the Jew who has been given the Law of Moses, or for the grace of the image of God resident in all people, including those who have not received the Law of Moses. They are judged according to what they know and do, not according to what they do not know and do not do:

> (Indeed, when Gentiles, who do not have the law, do by nature things required by the law, they are a law for themselves, since they show that the requirements of the law are written on their hearts, their consciences also bearing witness, and their thoughts now accusing, now even defending them.) This will take place on the day when God will judge men's secrets through Jesus Christ, as my gospel declares (vv. 14-16).

Paul says that judgment for those who have not heard the Gospel will be revealed through (the completed work of) Jesus Christ at the Last Day. What this means is that Jesus has the power to save those who acknowledge *nephesh* (needfulness) in the sight of creation, but whose historical situation precluded them from hearing and understanding the Gospel of Jesus. Their hearts cried out "Help me God!"

There is no salvation by any other means – only in the name of Jesus, and Jesus has the power to give ("grace") it to those who seek truth in spite of their sin. God's mercy trumps judgment for those who seek it.

The power of informed choice, vis-à-vis human lineages, is seen as Gentile nations derived from peoples who consciously chose dualistic evil, and the Jews derived from one man who was singular in his age, Abraham, who said yes to Yahweh and no to dualistic evil. Thus Gentile nations were far more deeply mired in sin since they lived and modeled it for generation after generation.

But in the final analysis, each person is judged according to what he has sought and done. Did he or she seek grace from the Creator, or self-sufficiency in his face? It is appointed for each of us to die once, then to face the judgment (see Hebrews 9:27); at that point the content of our hearts will then be made known. Will we love our Creator, and love who Jesus really is as we see him face to face, or will be choose the darkness of our own idolatries?

Predestination

In his Olivet discourse in Matthew 24 and Mark 13, Jesus spoke in terms of the "elect" – certain people were elected by God to receive the gift of salvation in the face of the coming tribulation. In Romans 11:28-29, Paul speaks of the Jews in terms of election, rooted in their nature as the chosen people through whom the Messiah would come.

This language of "the elect" begs the nature of "predestination." Jesus said to his disciples: "You did not choose me, but I chose you and appointed you to go and bear fruit – fruit that will last" (John 15:16). Yet all the disciples actively chose to say yes when Jesus called them, and this passage is specifically in reference to the 12 disciples. At that time, Jewish men who wanted to study the Torah chose which rabbi they wanted to learn under, if they were accepted.

Here Jesus was doing the choosing up front. He was no ordinary rabbi, and his mission was no ordinary mission.

How do we grasp this balance? The idea of predestination is most thoroughly covered by Paul in Romans 8-9. It is based on a concern of how Christians deal with suffering, and Paul's encouragement that "we know that in all things God works together for the good of those who love him, who have been called according to his purpose" (8:28).

Paul boldly declares that nothing can separate the believer from the love of Christ – whether the present or the future, angels or demons, etc. Thus Paul says, to paraphrase, "Hang in there – you are going to make it. How do I know that? Because God is sovereign, he is in control, you belong to him, and there is no power in all creation that can thwart his purpose – a purpose he ordained for you ahead of time. He is already where you are going to be, and he tells you that you made it."

Paul is strengthening the resolve of believers to faithfully endure trials, by rooting them in God's sovereign power and love. It is God's sovereignty that strengthens their power to make the right choices.

In Romans 8, as Paul uses the terms for "foreknow," "to know beforehand," "to predestine" and "to mark out beforehand," he is expressing his human perspective as a "jar of clay." Neither he nor any of us can ever access God's sovereign vantage point. To think we can describe God's sovereignty from his perspective is what happens when we try to defend God's sovereignty.

We cannot defend God's sovereignty – it defends our faith. We compromise God's sovereignty by bringing it down to the limitations of human understanding.

To predestine is to operate within the limits of space, time and number. Paul can use the language of predestination to describe God's activity on our behalf, because it is incarnational. Jesus became a man in order to relate to us, because we could not reach up and grasp God in his eternal nature. God relates to us in the use of predestination language because of its ethical purpose – to reflect God's power to give on our behalf, to encourage us to hang in there and be overcomers.

But whereas God can operate within the limitations of a human time line, as Lord of all, he is not bound by it. To abolish the real gift of human freedom and the power of informed choice in the name of God's sovereignty, as some are wont to do, is to bind God to a human time line and thus vitiate his sovereignty.

Sovereignty is God's domain and language, whereas choice is our domain and language – as a gift of the sovereign God in whom full freedom resides.

Space, Time and Number

C.S. Lewis defines an analogy that imagines a time line with God's universe around us. That line begins at the moment of biological origin, and ends at the moment of biological death. From whatever vantage point the present affords us, we can look back to our origins, and forward to our futures. Whereas we can remember some highlights of our past, and experience the present, we do not have any experiential knowledge of the future, only expectations. For myself, I can graph it this way:

1952/3 [conception/birth]   2011 [present]   2040 [future]

As a human being, I am finite and bound to the space-time continuum while in this mortal body. I have the power to make choices this day, influenced by the past and determinative for the present and future.

The covenantal name of *Yahweh* connotes the Divine Presence who transcends space and time – the "I AM WHO I AM" (Exodus 3:14), "who

141

is, and who was, and who is to come, the Almighty" (Revelation 1:8). The name of the Creator, *Elohim*, in its honorific plural qualities, transcends the concept of number.

Yahweh Elohim is greater than space, time and number, but the language of predestination is a creature of space, time and number. *Yahweh Elohim* is Present before my conception, Present at my conception, Present in my present, and Present in my future. It is all in his Presence, and as such the "pre" of predestination does not hold God hostage to the limitations of time. Since my future is in his Presence, God can speak out of that Presence into my present before I have experienced my future, encourage me to hang in there, declare that I will make it, in service to and not in violation the power of informed choice.

Since I am a creature of time, and my only presence is the time-bound present, with memory and hope, I cannot grasp the future as actual presence. But Yahweh is not bound, and he grasps all the past, present and future simultaneously as the I AM. When we as humans try to say that God predestines us apart from our full choice in the matter, we have made God into a creature of time, like a pagan deity; we have bound him to the limitations of human perspective, and have thus compromised his sovereignty.

To put it simply: God's sovereignty encompasses time, but time cannot grasp his sovereign nature. It is this perspective alone that can define predestination. In other words, here we are through no choice of our own, in the face of a beautiful creation, empowered to live, to love, to laugh and to learn. How can we but worship God?

God is sovereign, so we worship him; and we are free, so we are responsible – the essence of a godly character. If we know that God the Giver is sovereign, we will not become proud, thinking we can earn salvation. If we know that God the Giver has empowered us to make real choices with real consequences, we will be good stewards of his gifts.

The tension and balance here provides the "no excuse" of Romans 1:20 on the one hand, and the "choose this day" of Joshua 24:15 on the other. One without the other will produce an unbalanced faith. I can state with full integrity this paradox: I chose to believe in Jesus the Messiah – I could not choose otherwise. I said yes to Jesus' call to repentance (e.g., Mark 1:15), and left my former life to follow him, as did his original disciples. But too, Jesus chose me and I did not choose him (e.g., John 15:16). *Merismus*. His grace is truly irresistible for truth seekers.

What About Pharaoh, Jacob and Esau?

Well and good. But the question is often asked: What about Pharaoh? Does not the Scripture indicate that God's choice overrode Pharaoh's choice, and that God in effect predestined Pharaoh to go to hell?

In setting up this question in Romans 9, Paul first quotes Malachi 1:2-3, saying that God loved Jacob, but he hated Esau. Some might ask: "Is this not a form of prejudice?" For God chose Jacob, the younger of the twins, to take preeminence over Esau, before they were born, and before either of them did a good or bad deed. Again, if we grasp God's nature as being greater than space, time and number, then this language is clearly reflecting God's sovereign vantage point, which we cannot attain ourselves.

As well, Paul's point here is to articulate the just prerogatives of God in the face of human pretense. The "him who calls" (language in Romans 9) reflects the power to give. So also with "I will have mercy on whom I will have mercy." God gives mercy, and though we cannot grasp his eternal perspective, we can grasp the biblical reality where no one is ever judged apart from deeds they chose to do. Both Esau and Jacob fully experienced the power of informed choice.

In Genesis 25:1-34, we see Jacob was conniving, but too, Esau the skillful hunter could not wait an extra minute for a hot meal. As he came in from the open country, and wanted some of the stew Jacob was making, Jacob demanded that Esau sell him his birthright. "Look, I am about to die," Esau said, "What good is the birthright to me?" Esau could have found himself some other food easily – bread, vegetables, grains – without needing hot food. He had been sometime without hot food as it was. Instead, he "despised his birthright," a position of honor and privilege, in his momentary and lazy hyperbole.

He despised a birthright that was a gift of God, the blessing of his father as the firstborn, the largest inheritance in that culture, but especially the inheritance of the messianic promise through his father Abraham. To despise it was to despise, or hate, not only his father, Isaac, but likewise hate God as his heavenly Father; to reject God's goodness. Esau took a cavalier attitude toward God's blessings, similar to Cain's attitude toward God in Genesis 4. The use of the word "hate," in both the Hebrew and the Greek, literally means to "regard with less affection than" in the context of human relationships. It can then lead to abhorrence. This was Esau's attitude – he regarded God and his birthright with less affection than his belly in a moment of hunger. Thus God regarded Esau with less affection than Jacob, from Esau's perspective, and Esau knew he got what he deserved, what he had chosen.

As well, it is important to note that the "hate" of God toward Esau, recorded in Malachi, is contextually addressed to the Edomites, the nation that came from Esau, and hated the nation that came from Jacob, that is, the Israelites, even cheering on their enemies from the Exodus to beyond the

Babylonian exile. Too, this language says nothing about the salvation of Esau as a person. It is consistent with the power of informed choice.

Paul anticipates the proper concern with the justice of God: "Is God unjust? Not at all!" The power to give defines all. Thus Paul focuses on God's prerogative for mercy – his act of giving mercy to those of us who do not deserve it. To exemplify God's prerogative to show mercy, Paul cites Pharaoh.

The question is this: Is it fair to assume that the reference in Romans 9 to God hardening Pharaoh's heart means Pharaoh had no true choice in the matter? Once I tallied the number of clauses in Exodus 4-14 that refer to the hardening of Pharaoh's heart. There are various Hebrew verbs used that connote "strengthening," "hardening," "making heavy," and "yielding."

Depending on how clauses and references are calculated, the following balance emerges: 14 clauses where Yahweh took responsibility for Pharaoh's decision; 4 clauses where the language does not tell us who took responsibility; and 35 clauses where Pharaoh took responsibility for his own decision. A 5-2 ratio emphasizing human accountability.

Of the 14 clauses where Yahweh took responsibility, in 9 instances it specifically says he "hardened" Pharaoh's heart. Of the 35 clauses where Pharaoh took responsibility, in 4 instances it specifically says Pharaoh "hardened" his own heart. Then in verses like 10:27, we read the balance that Yahweh "hardened Pharaoh's heart, and he was unwilling to let them go."

In other words, Yahweh's sovereignty precedes and defines Pharaoh's fully owned choice – just as in the Garden of Eden with Adam. In Exodus 9:16-17, we read the passage that Paul quoted in Romans 9, as the balance is again in place:

> But I have raised you up for this very purpose, that I might show you my power and that my name might be proclaimed in all the

earth. You still set yourself against my people and will not let them go."

Or we can note the balance in Paul's words on Mars Hill, where God "determined the times set for them and the exact places where they should live ... so that men would seek him and perhaps reach out for him ..." (Acts 17:26-27). Sovereignty and choice, the latter made fully possible by the former. Pharaoh actively chose to oppose freedom and justice for the Israelites.

The showing of Yahweh's power to Pharaoh is his power to give. Egypt had forgotten the deliverance it received some 400 years earlier by the hand of Yahweh through Joseph, and the subsequent pharaohs enslaved Joseph's descendants with cruelty. In Exodus 4-14, Yahweh again and again gave Pharaoh the chance to relent from such cruelty, but he did not do so – he owned the choice to resist God, to resist his mercy. The judgment that Yahweh passed on Egypt was for their sin of despotic slaveholding, which was a derivative of their idolatry. Egypt mocked God by forgetting God's servant (Joseph) who had brought them deliverance in an earlier time, and now they compounded that sin by building their nation's wealth on the backs of Joseph's progeny.

Accordingly, when Paul alludes to Pharaoh in a context designed to emphasize the sovereign prerogative of God and his power to give, he assumes the reader's knowledge of Exodus 4-14, its antecedents, and the balance between sovereignty and choice found there. Pharaoh chose to be judged by God rather than relent his position of self-aggrandizing power – he loved the darkness rather than the light.

The Cosmic Risk

Finally, in this abbreviated review of the content of Romans 8-9, we come to what I call the "cosmic risk" taken by God, as I brushed by earlier. That is, God loves us enough to allow us to reject his love, for he loves us enough to risk those who refuse to believe for the sake of those who do believe.

But too often we think of risk in strictly human terms, in the sense of an investment that might not bring in its expected return, or one in which the principal could be lost. Not so in theological terms. In Matthew 25:14-30, in the parable of the talents, Jesus says that those who invest in the kingdom of God will gain the return proportionate to their ability and the risk they take. God is sovereign over his "markets."

In Romans 5:1-5, Paul speaks of a hope that has been honed by suffering, perseverance and character. It is a hope that "does not disappoint us" because of the reality of the Holy Spirit. Too often, we use the term "hope" not with its theological certainty, but in a sense of uncertain wishfulness.

The only risk we have in deciding to follow Jesus is that of losing worldly reputation, its material goods and therefore any false security they may bring. But if we know the Lord and the reality of the kingdom of God, this is no risk at all. In the parable of the man who found a treasure buried in a field, Jesus says that he went and sold all he had in order to buy that field (Matthew 13:44). He risked his whole material well-being in the certainty of knowing the treasure was there.

This is what we see reflected in Romans 9 (vv. 22-24) where God says he bears with patience "the objects of his wrath" for the sake of "his objects of mercy." He ethically treats all people the same – as Scripture says, he shows no favoritism (see Acts 10:34-35; Romans 2:9-11). He is willing that some are free to choose his wrath for the sake of those who choose his mercy. Satan and Pharaoh, even in their wickedness, remain servants of Yahweh (however unwillingly, in their exercise of the will to disobey). Yahweh is sovereign.

Yahweh's Sovereign Invitation for Abraham's Choice

When we consider the balance between sovereignty and choice, the question of prayer and its nature is crucial. Do we pray for something we cannot change? That would be a passive and puppet-like faith. Or do we believe that God's character can change due to our influence? That would be folly and idolatry.

God's character is that his sovereign goodness provides for our human freedom. As the Bible is examined across its pages, it is seen that all prayer involves spiritual warfare – as image-bearers of God, we are called to take our given authority over the demonic powers. We pray for their presence to be removed in the lives of people and nations, so that people can experience the level playing field to hear the Gospel, to choose between good and evil, as designed for Adam and Eve from the outset.

In reading Genesis 18:16-33, we enter a remarkable saga where Yahweh informed Abraham of the coming judgment on Sodom and Gomorrah. He was an image-bearer of God, called to judge between good and evil in Yahweh's sight. And yet Yahweh allowed Abraham to challenge the propriety of the judgment, and to negotiate the threshold down to the point that Yahweh would have withheld judgment had there been only ten righteous people in those cities. Here we see the power of informed choice, and the power to love hard questions (the substance of the next chapter), merge. We already noted the antithesis to Abraham with Bala'am in Numbers 22-24, where the same freedom of informed choice, grounded in reality, is given.

Yahweh does not change in his character (see 1 Samuel 15:29; Psalm 110:4; Malachi 3:6; Hebrews 7:21 and James 1:17); and Yahweh seeks people to repent and change, so that, consistent with his character, he can change prior outcomes they were enslaved by (see Jeremiah 18:7-10; Ezekiel 18:21-32).

The Power of Informed Choice

The power of informed choice, the gift of human freedom as defined in the biblical order of creation, is without comparison in its beauty, justice and mercy. Do we know it and live it in such a way that unbelievers are attracted to the Gospel by our witness?

The good news of the power of informed choice provides the seeds for theological maturity, and for political justice and mercy. We are called to announce the good news of the invitation to the feast of *akol tokel*, to the wedding supper of the Lamb in the politics of the kingdom of God to come.

♦ ♦ ♦

Chapter Four
The Power to Love Hard Questions

Three Strikes at Brown University

In the mid-1980s I was addressing a debate at Brown University. During the audience participation, a young woman posed me some of the most thoughtful questions I have ever received, from her politically "pro-choice" perspective.

After the debate, she approached me and said, "You know, John, before I came in here tonight, I hated you, even though I had never met you. You're a Christian, a man and pro-life." As she said this, I thought to myself, *Uh-oh, three strikes and you're out.*

She continued, "But you showed me more intelligence, respect and graciousness than any professor I've had in three years at Brown. Moreover, you posed to me questions I had never thought of before, and I just wanted to say thank you." She paused, took a breath and a step back, then said, "But that's not to say I'm converted yet!"

This is one of the most wonderful compliments I have ever received. This woman received a gift from me as a servant of the Gospel, and that gift was the freedom to ask questions.

In the 1989 debate at Brown, referenced earlier, I was asked some questions by a skeptical woman student. As we interacted, she concluded by asking, "Is there anything you don't know?" I said that there was much I don't know, and indeed, the more I learn, the more I realize how little I know compared with what there is to be known. By the same token, in terms of the subject at hand, I told her I had done my homework as thoroughly as possible.

A Feast of Exploration

The *akol tokel* of human freedom and the power of informed choice define an unlimited menu of good choices, and that menu includes an exploration of God's created order. The heavens and earth were made for Adam and Eve to "fill and subdue." To do so would require of them continual fellowship with God, and the freedom to think aloud in his presence, to ask questions. This we saw already with Abraham.

Before the advent of human sin, this thinking-aloud process would have been an endlessly delightful give and take between God and us, like little children in the presence of their father, discovering one wonder of the universe after another.

In the order of creation, the posing of questions among ourselves was in God's presence and ultimately directed to him, and it was meant to be natural and easy in terms of the process and access to the answers. Not that the answers did not require good and satisfying work. But there was meant to be no deleterious "sweat" on the man's brow or searing "pain" in childbearing for the woman. Work, expense of energy and a satisfying tiredness were to come with a productive day and week, and/or with the giving of birth. Rest was to follow – the joy of the Sabbath – in contemplation of the completion of something good, but not with anxious and burdensome exhaustion.

Thus, the posing of questions from the beginning was a feast of exploration, a purposed element in the freedom of *akol tokel*. It was the intrinsic excellence of the art of learning. In the redemptive context, as we face the need to overcome sin and the devil, questions become hard (e.g., Genesis 3:11ff with Adam and Eve's sin). They become hard because sin blinds us to our need to ask the right questions, and blinds us to a willingness to embrace the answers when change is required of us even if

151

the right questions are asked. And if we do not have God's grace to understand creation, sin and redemption, questions and answers are hard to grasp with intellectual clarity and honesty.

I once participated in a debate with the chairman of psychology at an Ivy League university, and it proved to be a gracious and intelligent interchange. At one juncture, he was exerting great intellectual energy in avoiding an obvious truth dealing with the biological humanity of the unborn. It hit me – so much intellectual energy can be spent trying to rationalize what the human soul knows is untrue, that clarity is lost and intellectual ability eventually avoids and does not pursue hard questions. They are often hard, not due to their intrinsic nature, but because the answers challenge deeply held presuppositions and chosen identities. Even for the most brilliant people.

Since questions become hard in the face of the reversal, we need to participate in the reversal of the reversal and embrace the power to love hard questions. To do so is to gain a level of freedom which is a character trait that welcomes the reality of the power of informed choice; and does not accept the deception of a misinformed choice which permits the justification of sin or of sloppy thinking.

In the Bible, the Lord God Almighty proves to be fully hospitable to our toughest questions. In contrast, non-biblical religion or secular constructs always place limitations on what questions are permissible – according to the vested interest of those who hold religious or political top-down power. Let's take a quick look at some key junctures of the biblical storyline in this respect.

The Queen of Sheba

In 1 Kings 10:1-9, we see how the Queen of Sheba traveled 1,000 miles north to pose King Solomon her hardest questions. He gave her the freedom to literally talk with him "about all that she had on her mind." In conclusion, she praised Yahweh Elohim, and his anointing of Solomon to "maintain justice and righteousness."

This event happened at the apex of Solomon's success and faithfulness to God, before he sinned egregiously in the building of a harem. In his later years he allowed some of his foreign wives to lead him to devotion to false gods, including the Ammonite god Molech, to whom child sacrifice was due. The power to love hard questions must never be put aside, or its prior fruit merely assumed, lest we also fail to finish the race and lose the prize ordained for us (see 1 Corinthians 9:24-27).

Jesus praised the Queen of Sheba in Matthew 12:41-42 for seeking out Solomon's wisdom, and then stated, "And now one greater than Solomon is here" (cf. Luke 11:31-32). In the context here, Jesus was responding to the hypocrisy of the Pharisees and teachers of the law who wanted him to perform a miraculous sign – almost as a sideshow. The Lord responded by aiming at their moral sin, namely, that they did not need to see a miracle to believe that Jesus was the Son of God. They had seen enough already, and the resurrection was coming.

The Jewish religious elitists, as the physical descendants of Abraham, thought that being the chosen people was a birthright that could not be lost. Thus, they were cocky in challenging Jesus. But Jesus corrected their self-deception, pointing out two situations where Gentiles sought out their Creator and, as a result, entered eternal life. The Ninevites were warned directly by God through a hesitant prophet (Jonah), and they repented. The queen of Sheba took her own initiative and traveled at great expense to seek out Yahweh, to ask hard questions of Solomon.

What If?

In Matthew 11:20-24, we read:

> Then Jesus began to denounce the cities in which most of his miracles had been performed, because they did not repent. "Woe to you, Korazin! Woe to you, Bethsaida! If the miracles that were performed in you had been performed in Tyre and Sidon, they would have repented long ago in sackcloth and ashes. But I tell you, it will be more bearable for Tyre and Sidon on the day of judgment than for you. And you, Capernaum, will you be lifted to the skies? No, you will go down to the depths. If the miracles that were performed in you had been performed in Sodom, it would have remained to this day. But I tell you that it will be more bearable for Sodom on the day of judgment than for you."

Jesus pointed out certain Gentile peoples as a reproving example to unbelieving Jews, this time in a "what if" scenario. Judgment begins with the household of God. He judged Korazin and Bethsaida, towns on the north shore of the Sea of Galilee, because they did not believe in Jesus when his power and nature had been made known to them. He judged Capernaum likewise, a much larger town in the same area that was also his hometown, and thus, its people were well familiar with him. In his judgment of Capernaum, Jesus used language reminiscent of Isaiah 14:12-15, where Yahweh judged the "king of Babylon" as the devil's surrogate who sought an exalted place of power above God.

Jonah preached to the Ninevites and they repented. The queen of Sheba sought out Yahweh through his servant Solomon, had her questions answered, and believed. But what about those in Tyre, Sidon and Sodom? Tyre and Sidon were trading cities in Philistia along the Mediterranean Sea, and the prophets Joel and Amos reproved them for selling captured Jews into slavery to Greece. And Ezekiel 28:1-9 profiles the king of Tyre as representing Satan. Then, Sodom's reputation was widely known for its social anarchy, including sexual perversions and the trampling of the poor and needy.

Thus, Jesus said that these people would have responded better than did these Jewish towns "if" they had had opportunity to see the miracles of Jesus. The Pharisees and Herod may have wanted to see miracles as a sideshow, but Jesus said, in contrast, that the pagans would have been interested in them as signs of the goodness and authority of the Lord. The slave traders in Tyre and Sidon would have repented and believed. The residents of Sodom would have at least restrained their wickedness enough to avert God's judgment. Thus, these peoples will face a more "bearable" judgment for deeds they did not do, but would have done, "if" they had been given the opportunity.

These are the words of Jesus, and they opens up a wide array of hard questions. For example, if God is just, why then did Tyre, Sidon, Sodom and Gomorrah not have an opportunity, as it were, to hear the words and see the miracles of Jesus? Also, what does it mean that here we see one people repenting, but the other people are not said to have repented – yet both gain a more "bearable" judgment?

Cain and the Beginning of Opposing Lineages

In the *moth tamuth* of the power of informed choice, God promised that sin would lead to the continual experience of death, to the brokenness of relationships. Following the reversal in the Garden of Eden, as mankind

155

propagated and spread across the planet, they did so with the freedom and accountability to reap what they had sown.

Very quickly the growth of wickedness begins in Genesis 4. Abel truly worshiped Yahweh, but Cain did not. Cain murdered him as a result, was banished from the "presence" of Yahweh to become a "wanderer," and his lineage traces down to a braggert, murderer and the first bigamist, Lamech, who exalted himself above Yahweh.

The purpose of Genesis 4-5 is to delineate the difference between those who chose or tried to choose the good (the lineage that led to the Messiah), and those who chose or acquiesced to evil (the lineage that leads to the antichrist). In Genesis 4 we also begin to embrace the hard questions about the outflow of the sin nature that commenced in Genesis 3. And we note that in Yahweh's employment of the "if" question with Cain (see 4:7), the father of the unrighteous fled the power to love hard questions.

The first question here involves the nature of worship. Cain was cavalier and Abel was principled. The distinction in the text is between Cain who "brought some of the fruits" versus Abel who "brought fat portions from some of the firstborn of his flock." The distinction is not between grain and meat, but between "some of" and "the best of." In other words, Cain was passive in his worship of God, and he was just going through the motions in a minimalist fashion, with no real thanksgiving for God's provisions. But Abel was active in his worship, offering Yahweh the best of the best, the prime rib as it were, as a statement of heartfelt thanks for Yahweh's provisions.

Cain knew this distinction and he became angry when he did not get away with it, and his face became downcast, turning away from the blazing fire (holiness) of Yahweh's full presence (the Hebrew term here is "face" – *panim*). This is the averted gaze of those who live in the darkness of their own chosen sins (no eyeball-to-eyeball power to live in the light). When

Yahweh confronted Cain with the hard question of his sin, he said that Cain would be accepted if he did what was right. In other words, doing what is right flows out of heartfelt worship, in trusting the goodness of Yahweh. Consistent with the power of informed choice, Yahweh said that Cain had the ability to choose the good and overcome the sin, but if he didn't, then sin would be crouching like the leopard at his door (as we noted earlier). Cain's choice to say no to the good was a choice to invite the devourer to leap on him.

When Yahweh made Adam and Eve, he gave them his best. They were made in his image to rule over the goodness of his creation. No higher goodness was possible for the original man and woman. This they naturally taught their children, and especially after they first reaped the fruit of sin. Abel learned it, and Cain refused, per their respective powers to choose. Because Cain would not worship God truly, he was despising the goodness of God. Since he did not acknowledge that Yahweh had given him his best, he did not give back to Yahweh his best. And thus he hated Abel, because Abel did thank God for the best he had been given, and gave back to God the best he had to offer.

Give and it will be given, or take and you will be taken. Since Cain was a taker and could not get away with it with Yahweh, he then became a taker of God's image, as he took Abel's life. As we treat God, so we treat our neighbor.

After the murder, Yahweh rhetorically asked Cain the whereabouts of his brother. When Cain pretended not to know, we learn how the pretension of ignorance is the weakest form of moral argument in history. Cain would not admit the truth and repent, because he was (damned) sure not to give up his self-sufficiency and self-righteousness; nor could he market a lie and say that Abel was at some other place and doing fine. So he pretended not to

157

know, just as the Pharisees did with Jesus when they would not, could not, answer a question without first repenting (see Matthew 21:23-27).

Cain, in a revealing profile of his sin, then posed a false question and asked Yahweh if he were his brother's keeper. It was the spiteful response of a murderer. There are questions that seek the truth – this is the power to love hard questions – and those that do not. Cain opposed the power to give, the power to live in the light, the power of informed choice and the power to love hard questions.

In Cain's chosen rebellion, he nonetheless complained about the deserved curse, complaining to Yahweh, "I will be hidden from your presence." But Cain was the one doing the hiding, as evident in his prior averted gaze.

So now we can grasp something of the moral nature of chosen sin, and how when worship of God is resisted, social evil is the result. Sin metastasizes culturally as *moth tamuth* becomes a reality. Not only in terms of the murder of Abel, and of Cain's subsequent wanderings, but especially in terms of his lineage. The balance of Genesis 4 chronicles in brief space the reality of how parents teach their children.

The fifth generation from Cain brings us to Lamech, who proudly celebrated his bigamy and power to murder, thus mocking the power to give, just as his ancestor Cain did when he would not give true worship to God. Instead of the man and woman becoming one flesh in mutually exclusive marriage, Lamech broke this boundary of freedom given in the order of creation. As well, instead of treating his first wife as his moral equal, he became the first misogynist ("woman-hater"), the first male chauvinist in recorded history. This was the original basis for polygamy, which in ancient culture was the prerogative of pagan kings

Lamech's evil only grew worse. Yahweh had earlier promised, in an act of redemptive grace, to protect the sinful Cain from anyone who would take vengeance on him for Abel's death, "seven times over." But Lamech took

Yahweh's prerogative of vengeance, and applied it not to the protection of others, but to his self-aggrandizing position. Namely, he declared he would avenge himself 77 times if a person even laid a hand on him. That is, he would avenge himself much more than Yahweh would, 77 as opposed to 7 times, thus elevating himself above God. And he bragged to his wives for having thus killed a man, a young man. Cain's sin was now magnified in his progeny.

At the end of Genesis 4, we have Seth's birth, and chapter 5 traces Seth's lineage through Noah. Seth replaced the fallen Abel, and he sought Yahweh faithfully. Cain's lineage, through Lamech, was the unfaithful one, from whom paganism traces its origins; and Seth's lineage was the faithful one leading to the Messiah. This portended a conflict as both developed culture, one using the resources of the image of God against God, the other in seeking God.

In Genesis 6:1-12, the sin of Cain and Lamech's lineage magnified further. The "sons of God" language in v. 2 confuses many. It does not refer to angels, for angels cannot marry and procreate. Rather it was a common designation for pagan kings who viewed themselves as the "sons of God" in a self-aggrandizing manner. Adam and Seth were sons of God literally (see Genesis 5:1-3; Luke 3:38), but submitted to the power to give.

The pagan "sons of God saw that the daughters of men were beautiful, and they married any of them they chose." In the Hebrew, a man having a sex with a woman means literally "to marry" her. The union of man and woman, once consummated, forever changes the dynamics between them. If marriage is rooted in mutual fidelity, then it is "very good." Otherwise it portends great brokenness and subsequent evil. Thus, here we have the pursuit of polygamy by the pagan kings, and the rejection of the power to give in godly marriage. So Yahweh declared judgment, "My Spirit will not contend with man forever, for he is mortal, his days will be a hundred and twenty years." This was a timeline until the judgment of the Flood, when Noah preached the coming judgment but no one listened outside his family.

Then the text follows with a mention of their offspring, the Nephilim (Hebrew for "fallen ones"), and how Yahweh "saw how great man's wickedness on the earth had become, and that every inclination of the thoughts of his heart was only evil all the time." The power to give had been replaced by the power to take, all rooted in forsaking the original power to give and receive in the image of God, where men and women are equals and complements, and marriage is monogamous and lifelong.

With sin having become the cultural norm, God was determined to work with the most faithful, with the "remnant." This was his purpose for Seth's line, which led to Noah, of whom the text says: "Noah was a righteous man, blameless among the people of his time, and he walked with God." He stood out hugely because a) he was a true son of God who walked with his heavenly Father, b) he was clearly a leader, and c) he maintained fidelity in his marriage.

Yet sin entered again with gusto after the flood, and became the norm once more. In redemptive history, one thing the Flood demonstrates is the power of sin upon human culture apart from God's grace. The planet was purged, but the human heart remained unpurged. External remedies will not cut it. Inward transformation is needed.

In the history of human culture subsequent to Noah, we see the same pattern that developed beforehand. Namely, most people fled God and eventually produced lineages ignorant of his covenant revelation to Adam and Noah, but never ignorant of God's testimony through the order of creation as Romans 1 says. The Lord allowed this to happen because of the power of informed choice where the power to procreate and influence our children is real. It is a blessing for the faithful to pass on what they know to "a thousand generations," but it is a curse which is passed on to "the third and fourth generation of those who hate me" (Exodus 20:5-6; Deuteronomy 5:9-10; 7:9-10).

God allowed this as a necessary consequence of his love with no strings attached. Therefore God did not force sinful cultures to listen to him. He let them go on their chosen ignorant ways, with their own chosen relationships; and many innocent offspring suffered as a result. But as well, many such offspring equally chose the evil they learned from their parents. Only God discerns the difference in response among those who have not heard the Word of God. This is where our hard question comes into play, as Jesus introduced the "what if" with regard to the "ignorant" people in places like Sodom and Tyre.

My Own Lineage

I can appropriate it this way. My surname is of Scottish descent, though I also have a good amount of English and Swedish elements in my blood. I am my mother's and father's child, and their genetic qualities, character traits and parenting decisions have invariably influenced me. And though there is much biblical faith in my lineage of which I know, I grew up in an agnostic Unitarian context.

Before the Gospel came to Europe, it was a primitive culture, like so many others, with the inability to restrain certain cruelties. But as the Gospel came, it broke the ignorant cycles, and so these dozens of generations later, the blessings have accrued to the descendants, even in spite of remaining issues, and among Scottish Presbyterians in my case.

So even though I was not raised to believe in Jesus as the Son of God, many ethical components such as honesty, education, hard work, thrift and aversion to the ego-turf concerns for "worldly reputation," have been deeply embedded in me by my father in particular. My mother instilled many good qualities in me as well, but she died shortly after I graduated from college, whereas my father is now 92.

This is to point out the power of the Gospel to break the "third and fourth generation" cycles of curses, and replace it with the cycles of "a thousand generations" of blessings. If a family line learns the blessings of what hard work produces – food, shelter, goods, safety, satisfying rest, etc. – then they have tasted some of the POSH Ls of the image of God. And these realities are not willfully discarded by the next generation, because of the blessings they provide. But curses are readily discarded when blessings are introduced into family lines – this is the power to give versus the power to take.

In the fall of 1996 I addressed a *Veritas Forum* at Harvard. A fellow Christian panelist was a medical doctor. She told a remarkable story of how she came to Christ in a third-world country. When she led her mother to Christ, the next morning her mother ran through the village praising Jesus. It was the first night in her life she was not plagued by demons. Such a blessing is far easier to pass on than the old curses.

Thus Again, What If?

This whole trajectory is examining the "what if" question that Jesus posed concerning Tyre, Sidon and Sodom. We are examining the justice of God. Very simply, God holds us accountable to what we know, no more and no less. But to whom much is given, much is required. God's power to give and the power of informed choice reflect the nature of genuine relationships, so he allows people to experience *moth tamuth* as they move away from his presence throughout history.

As our forebears reaped the fruit of sinful choices, they learned to admit their need, their *nephesh* in God's sight, apart from which salvation is not

162

possible. In order for Yahweh to restore right relationship to us, he demonstrated it in the specific community of the Israelites, who would come to know his goodness in relational intimacy. God found only a minority of sinful people who were willing to embrace such a relationship. He found Noah, and he found Abraham; and from Abraham came the covenant community of the Israelites that led to the Messiah, and the preaching of the good news to the Gentiles.

Tyre, Sidon and Sodom were among those peoples who had fled God, who rejected his revelation in the order of creation. The "what if" question is used by Jesus to highlight the rebellion of Jews in the covenant community. They should have known better and believed in their Messiah. And he was using it to indicate that, following his death and resurrection, the good news of God's love would be sufficiently demonstrated in history in order to redeem, for the Gentiles, the power of informed choice and call them to repentance.

Thus God is just and merciful. He is just in letting us choose our own destinies, as Tyre, Sidon, and Sodom had done. And he is merciful, knowing that sin robs the ability for complete justice in this world, and as such, people are victimized when born into sinful cultures. As Romans 1-2 makes clear, and as we have already reviewed, Gentiles without the law are judged by the content of their hearts in response to the clearly known God of creation, and this will be made known when they stand before him on the Last Day.

When we grasp the *merismus* of Scripture as it looks at this issue, we can understand why Jesus posed the hard question of the "what if" scenario about Tyre, Sidon and Sodom. God's power to give, and along with it, the power of informed choice, rooted in the order of creation, are consistent throughout the Bible.

These ethics alone exhibit the exquisite balance of justice and mercy, with the goal for mercy to triumph over judgment for all who believe. Paul identifies this balance in Romans 5:12-21, as he merges Adam's individual sin and accountability, with our passive inheritance of, yet active participation, in the same. We are our parent's offspring, whether with blessings or cursings, and yet we stand accountable for our moral choices individually before God, regardless of how many blessings or how much victimization we have experienced.

There are those who receive blessings and mock them; and there are those who receive blessings and honor them. There are those who suffer and grow more embittered against God as a result; and there are those who suffer and grow more humble and dependent upon God's mercy as a result. God alone knows the secrets of our hearts, and only the Bible provides the basis for a final and satisfying justice. What pagan origin text or religious and philosophical systems can compare with the reality and balance of the biblical witness, and the final triumph of goodness?

The Book of Job

The power to love hard questions continues to surface throughout Scripture. The book of Job celebrates the freedom God gives us to wrestle with hard questions. Job suffers – through no fault of his own, as Yahweh allows Satan to tempt him – to demonstrate to the devil the nature of true faith.

In the process of Job's sufferings, the human heart was laid bare, and he was free to pour out his toughest questions to Yahweh, and to his "counselors."

Job's three friends, Eliphaz, Bildad and Zophar, were reproved by God, because in the end they grew proud against Job in their posing of questions.

Elihu was not reproved, because while asking hard questions of Job, he did not grow proud against him. When God answered Job, he did so with a host of questions that only the sovereign Yahweh can answer, and he did not chastise him per se, as Job confessed his humility. And because of Job's humility in God's sight, rooted in the power to love hard questions in the sight of Yahweh, all his fortunes were restored and Satan was vanquished.

The Book of Psalms

The power to love hard questions is highlighted in the book of Psalms. It has been titled by one scholar *Out of the Depths* because of its focus on the reality of broken relationships, and the emotional, physical and spiritual stresses that result. So many hard questions we deal with are indeed intellectual, and Scripture addresses them. But intellectual questions are in truth never divorced from relational or emotional issues. The Psalms are universally loved, and especially Psalm 23 – they minister to the souls of all of us, for we all know heartache.

One example of a tough question is the anguish in Psalm 22:1, "My God, my God, why have you forsaken me?" The rest of the psalm chronicles David's pain and sense of total abandonment as a result of the hatred of his enemies, and ends with victory. It is also a messianic psalm that portrays many elements of the crucifixion. In fact, when Jesus hung on the cross, he cried out these words (see Matthew 25:46; Mark 15:34).

Some skeptics see Jesus confessing doubt in God at this moment. However, the truth is entirely different. Jesus knew he was to die as "the Lamb of God" (John 1:29), according to the Levitical requirements for the atonement of sins. Jesus was to die in our stead, paying sin's penalty so as to rescue us from its debt. In 2 Corinthians 5:21, Paul says, "God made him who had no sin to be sin for us, so that in him we might become the righteousness of God." Sin by definition is the brokenness of relationship with God, the absence of his (full) presence. In Isaiah 59:2, it says that God hides his presence from our sin.

In other words, Jesus had to become as utterly forsaken as sin itself in order to experience our pain and redeem us from it. He had to be utterly abandoned by his Father. So when he cried out David's anguish, "My God, my God, why have you forsaken me?" he was not questioning or doubting God. Rather he was touching the depth of human anguish represented in Psalm 22:1, and the Jewish bystanders knew exactly what he was quoting, though not yet its significance. The hardest questions born in human anguish were pressed to the lips of Jesus at this moment. As he identified with David's abandonment, he became a sin offering for us.

The Book of Ecclesiastes

In the book of Ecclesiastes, we see the words of "the Teacher," likely Solomon, who speaks of the vanity or meaninglessness of life when people pursue "wisdom" and "projects" apart from the knowledge of God, when pleasure for its own sake becomes an idol. Solomon knew well his sins, and concluded Ecclesiastes this way:

Now all has been heard;

here is the conclusion of the matter:

Fear God and keep his commandments,

for this is the whole duty of man.

For God will bring every deed into judgment,

including every hidden thing, whether it is good or evil

(12:13-14).

The words in the Book of Ecclesiastes reflect the literary device of a man who knew better to begin with, who nonetheless indulged in folly, and emerged afterward knowing better what he knew better to begin with. Thus the Teacher's purpose in Ecclesiastes was to think aloud in retrospect, and to embrace hard questions, but not from a prescriptive or dogmatic teaching style. Rather, he invited the reader, including any skeptic, to experience the process with him. This is an intellectually sophisticated way of embracing the power to love hard questions, and it is a means that respects and catalyzes the image of God in all of us. We learn far more by entering into a story where we are challenged to think on our own in the sight of God and one another, than when we are given atomistic bits of knowledge to passively swallow.

Jeremiah

The power to love hard questions is also highlighted in a freedom Jeremiah experienced to pour out his complaint to Yahweh, much in the flavor of the Psalms. Jeremiah was called by Yahweh to be a prophet from before his conception, and he was the final prophet in Jerusalem before the Babylonian captivity in 586 B.C. He knew his calling and was faithful to it. In chapter 19, Jeremiah prophesied, in the presence of the people and priests, against the child sacrifice that was increasing in Jerusalem during its final days. As a result, the priest and chief officer of the temple, Passhur, had Jeremiah beaten and placed in prison. After Jeremiah was released, and after he prophesied against Passhur, he was free to complain to Yahweh in 20:7-18.

In so doing, he charged that Yahweh deceived him, and accordingly suffered ridicule and mockery for preaching the truth. Then he switched gears and praised Yahweh, but then lapsed again into cursing the day he was born. The agony is palpable.

How many of us have ever screamed out to God, even believing he has somehow deceived us? Do we realize the level of freedom we have in his presence to pour out the anguish of our hardest questions, knowing that he will receive us? The word for "deceive" as translated by the NIV comes from the common Hebrew term *patah*, which means to "open wide." In the moral sense, this refers to being opened and exposed, laid bare and vulnerable. In other words, Jeremiah was saying that God was mocking his faithfulness to the ministry by exposing him to such suffering and public humiliation. Because his friends claimed he was being deceived, after his prophetic pronouncement against child sacrifice, Jeremiah wondered why Yahweh allowed it. Was Yahweh in fact the One deceiving him, opening him wide and laying him bare before friends and enemies alike?

The Bible is straightforward and candid in portraying the humanity of its saints – no mythologies here. The turmoil in Jeremiah's soul was laid bare so that we can all see the process of how God works "this treasure in jars of clay." If we refuse to confront painful and hard questions in our lives, then we run from reality, and we run from the healing that the answers will provide.

As Jeremiah screamed out to Yahweh his complaint, he also noted the inescapability of fulfilling his mission – the fire in his bones of God's Word that must be released. Here the true balance of the power of informed choice is evident – God's sovereign calling and our full participation. As I noted the paradox last chapter, "I chose to believe in Jesus the Messiah – I could not choose otherwise," so too Jeremiah (and prior) chose to obey Yahweh's call on his life – he could not choose otherwise. The Scripture takes all this in stride, portraying a prophet who suffered for doing what is right and who had the freedom in Yahweh's sight and in the sight of the nation, to not only ask Yahweh hard questions, but to challenge him head

168

on in his sinful anguish. God is so sovereign that we have the freedom to embrace the power to love hard questions.

The Books of Jonah and Habakkuk

In the book of Jonah, the prophet was called to preach to the pagan Ninevites. Since Jonah hated them too much to do so, Yahweh had to teach him a series of hard lessens, and by the end of the book, Jonah still did not get it. So Yahweh concluded the book with a hard question of Jonah: "Should I not be concerned about the great city?"

Habakkuk was a contemporary of Jeremiah, and likewise bore faithful witness to Yahweh in the final generation before the Babylonian exile. His short book is actually a dialogue with Yahweh, where he starts off in distress over the evil and apostasy in the nation of Judah, and wonders why Yahweh is not punishing these sins. Yahweh answers by saying that the ruthless Babylonians are coming, i.e., as a measure of judgment against Judah's sins. Habakkuk could not understand how Yahweh would use a people more wicked than Judah to punish Judah, so he posed a second set of questions. Then Yahweh answered by saying that Babylon would also be judged thereafter. Habakkuk thus concluded by praising Yahweh in the face of his trials, knowing the power to overcome is given to those who embrace such a faithful power to love hard questions.

Jesus' Teaching Style

In his earthly ministry, Jesus taught in classical rabbinic style – posing more questions (some 188 different questions in the gospels) than giving answers, and inviting people to join him in the experience of shared stories. He would mix references to biblical history with parables where he would tell a story applicable to all, and rooted in the common knowledge of daily life. It is such a Hebrew ethic of communication that allows people to first own the questions, apart from which they cannot own the answers.

The authority of Jesus was evident to those whom he touched, but for his enemies, he allowed the power-to-love-hard-questions process to expose their true intentions. The power to ask good questions helps us discern between truth and falsehood, and to see people's true motivations revealed. And Jesus knows it best.

This is seen during Passover Week (see Matthew 21-23; Mark 11-12; Luke 19:28-20:47). After Palm Sunday, Jesus engaged in a debate with the religious and political elitists who opposed him, in the Court of the Gentiles, the outer court of the temple where Gentiles were welcome, in the presence of large crowds. This debate was catalyzed with his healing of the blind and the lame, in response to which the children started enthusiastically shouting in the temple courts, calling Jesus the "Son of David," a messianic title. His enemies challenged his allowance for such a claim, and Jesus responded with a question that partially quoted another messianic prophecy.

Being flustered by this question, his enemies returned the next day with an attempt to trap Jesus in his words. So they posed a series of questions, not out of a love for honest questions, but by prostituting questions into a falsehood and smokescreen against Jesus' true questions. Jesus answered them with rhetorical questions that they could not or would not answer, because to do so would expose their dishonesty. At the end of the process, they dared not ask him any more questions, and the people were delighted. Jesus embraced the power to love hard questions as his strength, and the enemies of the Messiah fled it.

As a result, Jesus was proven blameless as the Lamb of God in the sight of all, having given his enemies a level playing field to challenge him, and was able to die on the cross, blameless in the sight of his enemies, able therefore to pay the debt of sin once and for all. This is the fruit of the power to love hard questions – our very salvation. In fact, in this debate, Jesus highlighted all six pillars of biblical power.

This storyline is looked at in detail in my book, as referenced earlier, *Jesus, in the Face of His Enemies*.

Paul's Teaching Style

In Acts 17:16-34, Paul stopped in Athens en route from Berea to Corinth, awaiting Silas and Timothy, to join him. In this interim period, he naturally engaged his intellect and the power to love hard questions. His soul was grieved by the city's plethora of idols, so he talked with the Jews and God-fearing Gentiles in the synagogue, and the pagans in the *agora* – the highly trafficked marketplace in the center of the city. And it was here that the Stoics and Epicureans, de facto secularists unable to transcend the religious ethics of their own culture, also engaged with him in discussion. They thus invited him to address a meeting of the Areopagus, the leading institution at that time for pagan worldviews. The Areopagus comes from the Greek for "hill of Ares," and Ares was the Greek god of war. The Latin translation is "Mars Hill," since Mars is the Roman god of war.

Paul was already educated in Greek culture. He took opportunity to refer to the altar of "an unknown god" as a place where the image of God within them would be receptive to his preaching. From there he proclaimed the one Creator, for whom all cultures have some recollection and recognition, as well as an awareness that we have all descended from one man – from Adam. This was a powerful statement that separates biblical faith from all pagan understandings – biblical faith is rooted in verifiable history, not myth, with written genealogies tracing all the way back to the creation of man.

Thus he honed in on the crucial difference of worshiping the Creator versus worshiping the creation with idols created by our own hands – the central distinctive between Jewish and pagan religion. Then Paul quoted Cretan, Cilician and Greek poets who acknowledged the one Creator, but did not know his true name and nature. In so doing, Paul anchored the reality of the one God in the language of their own culture, redemptively applying devotion to a false god who had a quasi-creator status (Zeus), to devotion to the true Creator (Yahweh Elohim) – for those so willing.

The power of informed choice was ratified in terms of the accessibility we all have to God, and demonstrated as God overlook the ignorance of paganism. But now the accountability was to repent because of the resurrection of "the man he has appointed" to judge the world. The evidence was the resurrection, and as Paul understatedly referred to both Adam and Jesus in terms that ratified the humanity of the Greek skeptics.

What I enjoy about this incident so much is Paul's preparedness at a moment's notice to speak to anyone, anywhere, about his faith. In an overlapping context, Jesus says to his disciples:

> "You must be on your guard. You will be handed over to the local councils and flogged in the synagogues. On account of me you will stand before governors and kings as witnesses to them. And the gospel must first be preached to all nations. Whenever you are arrested and brought to trial, do not worry beforehand about what to say. Just say whatever is given you at the time, for it is not you speaking, but the Holy Spirit" (Mark 13:9-11).

In this passage in Luke, we see additional elements:

> "But before all this, they will lay hands on you and persecute you. They will deliver you to synagogues and prisons, and you will be brought before kings and governors, and all on account of my name. This will result in your being witnesses to them. But make up your

mind not to worry beforehand how you will defend yourselves. For I will give you words and wisdom that none of your adversaries will be able to resist or contradict" (21:12-15).

Jesus also taught a parable that has applicability here:

He said to them, "Therefore every teacher of the law who has been instructed about the kingdom of heaven is like the owner of a house who brings out of his storeroom new treasures as well as old" (Matthew13:52).

Paul experienced all that Jesus warned about, but the council on Mars Hill no longer had political authority, since Rome ruled. It now met primarily for philosophical and religious debate. In being called on to answer for his faith, Paul was free to go without a prepared speech, drawing out of the storeroom of his preparedness something "old" (the order of creation) and something "new" (his reference to the altar of an unknown god). He depended on the Holy Spirit in the moment to deliver the right message – and with a wisdom that could not be contradicted, just as Stephen demonstrated in Acts 7 on a moment's notice.

When Jesus told his disciples not to be anxious beforehand about what to say, he also assumed their intimate knowledge of the Hebrew Scriptures and a living relationship with God the Father through him, upon which the Holy Spirit would draw. We are called to embrace the power to love hard questions and the work of preparedness it naturally involves, to be fully available to the work of the Holy Spirit through us. It means that like a good athlete, as Paul speaks of in 1 Corinthians 9:24-27, we will have disciplined our minds and bodies relentlessly, so that when the time comes to run the race, we will run our best.

And as did Paul in Athens, we also need to know the culture in which we seek to bear witness. Paul knew all the questions, and the Greek philosophers wrestled with these same common human questions as well as

173

any pagans did. Paul was adroit enough to address them at a moment's notice because he was disciplined in the power to love hard questions.

Paul was trained as a rabbi, and the rabbinic teaching style involved a constant dialogue centering on shared questions, of a constant give and take. He was rabbinic in his 13 New Testament letters to believers, and likewise in Athens. In his more didactic moments, even when speaking emphatically about what is right and wrong, he was always based on the Hebrew ethic of dialogic communication in the context of shared stories – not in one-way diatribes. In Romans 9, he posed and answered questions with which he knows his readers were interacting. In the context of some difficult cultural and theological disputes in Romans 14, e.g., kosher versus Gentile diets, and the Sabbath being limited to one day as opposed to being a greater concept, Paul inserted into the debate, as he gave his instructions: "Each one should be fully convinced in his own mind" (v. 5). This is the power to love hard questions – we cannot own the answer to a question unless we first own the question.

God invites us into his presence to pose our hardest questions, and the church should likewise be hospitable, aggressively so, to believers and unbelievers alike.

Acid Tests of Integrity

Thus far in these pages, we have touched base with many hard questions. I believe that the more humble we are in seeking God for answers to hard questions, the more we can begin to grasp the answers he has for us, and thus grow in wisdom. The more we grow in wisdom, the more we should naturally grow in unfeigned humility. And the product will be greater conviction, greater competency, greater love for others and a greater freedom to admit that we do not know the answer when indeed we do not know. Abolition of pretense. We cannot know the mysteries that require Yahweh Elohim's eternal perspective, but we can come to learn all that is within his universe as he reveals it to us; and in the gift of eternal life, as we have forever to explore it.

In our *Sacred Assemblies for the Unborn* at New England's largest abortion center, Preterm, from 1989-1991, an important component of our strategy was a commitment to communication, face to face, with abortion-rights activists. They were from the Boston chapter of the NOW and other allied organizations. They had recruited many students from the college campuses, acting in counter-demonstration to our presence.

In the fall of 1989, I had four students from Gordon-Conwell Theological Seminary doing "field education" under my supervision. One student, Andy Davis, now a pastor with a Ph.D. in Church History, was in charge on a given Saturday in October. Andy was holding a sign next to several abortion-rights activists, each holding their signs, and he sought to initiate conversation. One college-age woman conversed with him for some 45 minutes, but in a distant fashion. NOW had told their recruits not to engage in conversation with us, saying that we had an ulterior agenda to eventually surprise them, rush in and physically block access to the abortion center. This we were theologically opposed to doing, but NOW did not yet trust that to be the case. In other words, this woman was committed to being there since we were there, and perhaps the conversation helped her pass the time.

At one point she asked Andy a question, and Andy said something like, "That is a good question, and I really don't know the answer. I'll have to get back to you." This freedom to admit when we do not know the answer highlights integrity in the power to love hard questions – in this case, it was not having the right answer per se as much as having a genuine and humble love that made the difference. This woman was astonished at his honesty, and then entered into a warm and truly probing discussion, and two of her friends joined in as well. For the next 45 minutes, they discussed one question: Who is Jesus Christ?

Andy communicated across the chasm. More remarkably yet, this woman returned to Preterm five months later looking for him. He was not there, so she asked the seminary student in charge that day, Bill Wilder, earlier referenced, how she could contact him, and Bill provided the information. Her statement went something like this, "Where is that fellow I talked with in October? He asked me a couple of questions that have been bugging me ever since, and I need to talk with him."

In another acid test of integrity, imagine someone asking you if you would like U.S. law to require people to be put to death if they engage in homosexual acts. What would be your gut level response? No, of course. But then, how do we deal with Leviticus 20:13?

> If a man lies with a man as one does with a woman, both of them have done what is detestable. They must be put to death; their blood will be on their own heads.

In 1994, I was invited to debate Mel White on the radio. Mel is the former ghostwriter for people such as Billy Graham, Pat Robertson and Jerry Falwell, and a former professor at Fuller Theological Seminary. Then he divorced his wife, claiming he was born homosexual, and moved in with a male partner. He also claimed still to be an evangelical Christian, and that the evangelical church has sinned against him and fellow homosexuals who live in "committed relationships" by not accepting them. He reverses the language of Sodom and Gomorrah in Genesis 19, and says the sins of the Sodomites were a matter of being "inhospitable" more than being concerned with homosexuality. Thus, he reasons that evangelical Christians today who do not accept him as "a stranger at the gate" are, at least by implication, the true Sodomites.

Mel asked me this very question on live radio, saying that if I took the Bible literally, I must believe that homosexual persons should be put to death. I answered by showing how those who would commit homosexual acts in ancient Israel would do so as an act of political treason against Yahweh – a capital offense (among other capital offenses) against the nation where Yahweh was King. If any Israelite wanted to commit homosexual acts, all the pagan nations surrounding Israel would allow it in some form or another. He could leave Israel anytime and go to a pagan nation. In fact, the Law of Moses and the ancient Israelite nation were the only religion and culture that then said a categorical no to homosexuality.

At a deeper level, the nature of a biblical theocracy, as we have already defined, is rooted in informed choice. Moses and Joshua were clear – they could choose whether or not to serve Yahweh, and Yahweh had proven his goodness ahead of time. The Israelite theocracy existed only in a certain period of time as a political wall of protection against the enemies of the messianic lineage. That season a) ended with the Babylonian exile, and b) was fulfilled when Jesus came the first time as Messiah and Suffering Servant. Thus, before anyone chose to live in or remain in theocratic Israel, he or she had to first agree that the Law of Moses was good, and it was intended for the protection of their lives, liberties and properties.

There are only two biblical theocracies in history – from Moses to Jeremiah, and when Jesus returns as the reigning King. Both theocracies are by definition "communities of choice."

Thus, our calling as Christians in this age between the two theocracies is to affirm the unalienable rights of all persons equally, including homosexual persons; but none of us can injure the life, liberty or property of another person without being accountable to the law, in all directions. And for homosexual persons, and in all their struggles, we celebrate the preaching of Jesus, repentance and deliverance through the power of the Holy Spirit, and the invitation to citizenship in the kingdom of God.

But if they choose homosexuality over the Gospel, then they will face judgment on the Last Day, as will all people who deliberately refuse God's Word and goodness. No one is forced into eternal life. Thus, I will defend the unalienable rights of a homosexual person, not because he or she is homosexual, but because we are all made in the same image of God. The good news of Jesus is that he loved us when we were his enemies in unbelief, so that we can become his friends in turning to him. We invite homosexual persons to repent and join the kingdom of God, but we force nothing.

Mel said it was the most Christian answer he ever heard, as I articulated it then, and that he and I would burn up the telephone wires debating the Scriptures. But after the radio show, he cut off any further communications. He was offered generous compensation to debate me at Coral Ridge Presbyterian Church in Fort Lauderdale, Florida, at Dr. James Kennedy's personal invitation. But he said no, even though he had protested at Kennedy's church before, at Jerry Falwell's church and at Pat Robertson's CBN headquarters. Even yet, in his most recent email to me in 2004, he said that for some reason he could not help liking me. The truth can be spoken in love, if we are fully biblical.

The Power to Love Hard Questions

Life presents us with hard and painful questions. If we run from them, we will be tackled. If we run at them, we will be overcomers.

If the power to love hard questions can infect the church significantly, we will become increasingly revived, reformed, transformed and equipped to turn this culture right side up, to reverse the reversal enough to give society a taste of the power of the age to come. None of us can possess the answer to a question we have not asked; and so often the key to enabling people to ask the right questions of God is to allow them the freedom to ask of us any and all questions on the terms they choose. We can then be aggressive in our hospitality to the toughest question of skeptics. Our listening love becomes God's instrument to draw them to the right questions, and to the Source for the answers.

♦ ♦ ♦

Chapter Five

The Power to Love Enemies

A Marxist-Leninist at Street Level

On June 3, 1989 at our first *Sacred Assembly for the Unborn* at Preterm, at which hundreds of people were present, the largest banner of the abortion-rights activists said, "Oppose the oppression of working women." Below it was the larger main slogan: "Fight the Reaganite Anti-Abortion Movement!" On the bottom it said, "Marxist-Leninist Party." The man in charge of the banner learned that I was the organizer of the Christian pro-life group involved, made his way over to me, introduced himself as secretary for the Marxist-Leninist Party of Boston, and wondered with open hostility if I were a "Reaganite anti-choice clone." From there he lectured me for up to 30 minutes, in language laden with Marxist nomenclature and assumptions.

He was a large man, and as I listened to him, I found many points where I could have easily raised objections. But instead I remained silent on those divisive points and affirmed with nods or brief words the various places where I agreed. Toward the end of this time, he suddenly realized that I was listening to him – and was visibly shocked. His presumed stereotype of me was wrong, and he perceived the respect I gave him as an individual.

Our conversation was interrupted by some exigency as we stood among so many people on the sidewalk and street. Some time later, he approached me again, but this time with an eagerness for a true exchange of ideas. We talked, and I made my arguments for a biblical worldview and its pro-life perspectives, and soon he was beginning to ask me question after question. Again the conversation was interrupted. At the end of the morning, he approached me a third time and said, "I have just one more question." I forget the exact question he posed, but it had something to do with how Christians should conduct themselves in political disputes, and my answer was simple and straightforward. Then he broke into a big smile, shook my hand with the strength of a rail-splitter, said "thank you," and left.

The power to love hard questions paves the way for the power to love "enemies." Initially, this man regarded me as the "enemy." But from my perspective I have no "enemies" who are human beings. My only enemies are the devil and his demons. But there are those who are enemies of the Gospel, or who at least they think they are. It all depends whether or not they understand the true Gospel, and if they have been burned by betrayal or hypocrisy in the name of the church or Christianity.

The Most Effective Lesbian Activist in Massachusetts

On November 22, 2002, I addressed a Mars Hill Forum at Boston University with Arline Isaacson, co-chair of the Massachusetts Gay and Lesbian Political Caucus. Our topic was "Is Same-Sex Marriage Good for the Nation?" Arline is the most effective homosexual-rights lobbyist in the state, and has been so since the late 1980s.

I arrived in the auditorium before Arline did, and when she came in, I immediately introduced myself, smiled, shook her hand and said, eye to eye, that it was a pleasure to meet her. She had a coterie of lesbian and male homosexual friends with her, and when they saw how easily and genuinely I greeted Arline, some of them were clearly shocked – even lurching back. In other words, the stereotype of an evangelical minister was that I must be "homophobic," that is, fearful of being in the presence of homosexual persons, and clearly hateful toward them. Not so here.

During Arline's introductory comments, she stated that every other person she debated on this subject "had palpably hated me, but not so tonight with John Rankin." I was unprepared for this remark, and whether Arline had concluded this beforehand, or whether my eyeball-to-eyeball welcome made the difference, I do not know.

That evening I made a concerted presentation for the goodness of man and woman in marriage, "one man, one woman, one lifetime," chastity outside of marriage and fidelity within. On such a basis I said an unambiguous no to same-sex marriage. During her opening comments, Arline spoke of her lesbian partner of many years, and how they had two artificially inseminated children. These children were Arline's biological children, conceived through anonymous sperm donors.

Then during our dialogic period, I said that I was going to ask her a personal question, which she did not have to answer if she considered it too probing. I asked her what she would say to her children when they were old enough to ask, "Who is my daddy?" and "Where is my daddy?" Arline said she had not thought of that question and would have to cross that bridge when she came to it. I left it there, open-ended.

During the question and answer period, in the midst of an energetic moment with a questioner from the audience, Arline looked at me and said, "We know that you love us John." She had a good number of friends there, and most of the 225 or so people were on her side of the question. Yet I had never used the explicit language of "love." Rather I had shown Arline full respect as an image-bearer of God in the face of a most divisive debate.

On March 20, 2005, we addressed the same question at Harvard. Here I was explicit in my critique of the trajectory of the 2004 *Goodridge* ruling of the Massachusetts Supreme Judicial Court legalizing same-sex marriage. It lifted same-sex marriage to the threshold of "fundamental" and "basic rights," even parallel to those of unalienable rights. This will ultimately trump religious liberty and destroy civil liberties for all people, as it sets a human definition of rights above those of the Creator. This argument remains untouched historically and legally speaking, and as the argument by same-sex marriage advocates most often is emotional in nature. Subsequent court rulings only ratchet up this trajectory.

During the question and answer period, Arline pointedly challenged me, "John – why are you trying to harm me and my family" by opposing same-sex marriage? I was incredulous, given our honest rapport prior to this point (and afterward as well). So I said something like, "That is remarkable. You and your partner have been together long before same-sex marriage was a legal possibility, and you had your artificially inseminated children years before it was a possibility. The ones doing the harm are the male chauvinists who sold their sperm for fifty bucks and don't give a damn."

Now this is virtually the most confrontational thing I have ever said in a Mars Hill Forum (other than with the reprehensible Fred Phelps of "God Hates Fags" repute). Yet as I did, Arline and the audience raised no objection, and we moved on. In other words, when we truly love those who might be considered by some as "political enemies," we are greatly empowered to speak the truth – even when it is uncomfortable. In fact, Arline and I addressed another forum in 2008, and at the end of it she gave me a hug. And later she said to me that I was a "true gentleman and a thoughtful advocate." In other words, the purpose of the Gospel is not to win a debate in order to win a debate, but to win an honest relationship. This means the freedom to invest trust in the other person in spite of our deepest differences, and on the assumption that we are all made for trust, having been made in the image of God. This will always advance the Gospel.

The Apex of the New Covenant

In the Sermon on the Mount, Jesus sets forth the ethical code necessary to fulfill the Law of Moses – a code only he could live up to as the Messiah. But with his completed work on the cross, and in the resurrection and ascension, he gave the covenant of the Holy Spirit to those who believe, so that the grace of God can flood our lives and renew our minds to walk in his ways (see 1 John 2:3-6). The highest and most exacting point of the Sermon on the Mount, its theological apex, is the power to love enemies. In Matthew 5:38-48, Jesus challenges the disciples to put aside "an eye for an eye" ethic (*lex talionis* – "law of equal payment"), and learn to "turn the other cheek," walk the extra mile, love our enemies and pray for those who persecute us.

In Exodus 21:23-25 and elsewhere we find the language of "an eye for an eye." This language describes accountability, where if someone deprives someone else of an eye, he owes him for that loss. And this debt is taken care of through redemptive payment, to make up for the injured man's financial loss. Never once in Israelite or Jewish history was an eye gouged out for such payment. Its idiomatic use was clear. In the Sermon on the Mount (see Matthew 5:27-31), in the context of adultery and lustful eyes and groping hands, Jesus says to gouge out the eye or cut off the hand rather than risk hell. But as he later makes clear (see Matthew 15:1-20), sin comes from within the heart, and sin can only be dealt with, eventually, by the circumcision of the heart – the language of baptism (see Colossians 2:11-17). In other words, he was using clear hyperbole that everyone knew.

Jesus came to fulfill the Law of Moses and introduce the New Covenant, which transfers us from the outer code of the Law to the transformation of the inner person (see the argument in Hebrews 9), from the *quid pro quo* status of *lex talionis*, to the unilateral power to love enemies. In the Sermon

184

on the Mount, Jesus ratchets up the redemptive power and places radical choices before those who would believe in him. Part of his fulfillment of the Law also required its proper definition. His reference to the saying "love your neighbor and hate your enemy" was not a quote from the Old Testament, but rather it was a quote of a perverted opinion that had become accepted among the post-exilic Jews.

Turn the Other Cheek, Walk the Extra Mile

When Jesus teaches us not to resist an evil person, but instead to turn the other cheek, it does not refer to pacifism in the face of evil. The Greek word in play, to "strike," refers to an open-handed or backhanded slap, in order to induce shame, to publicly humiliate. In the ancient Middle East, and up to the present, it is a culture where honor and shame play central roles. If a person has not acted honorably, according to the standards at hand, then deliberate shame can be visited upon him. And the shame can be so intense culturally that shamed people will oftentimes despair of life. So this is at least part of the context to which Jesus addressed his words. In Hebrews 12:2, the writer speaks of Jesus, "who for the joy set before him endured the cross, scorning its shame..." This reality can be seen explicitly in the messianic prophecy in Isaiah 50:6-7:

I offered my back to those who beat me,
my cheeks to those who pulled out my beard;
I did not hide my face
from mocking and spitting.
Because the Sovereign LORD helps me,
I will not be disgraced.
Therefore have I set my face like flint,
and know I will not be put to shame.

What we see here is a fierce resistance to false shame, a fierce scorning of it, a rejection of the accusations rooted in the accuser – the ancient serpent and his proxies. The messianic prophecies in Isaiah 42-53 have extraordinary detail that we see fulfilled in the gospels as Jesus goes to the cross. So as Jesus turned his back to the scourges, and his cheek to those who pulled out his beard, he was resisting the devil at a remarkable level. He would not condescend to the level of responding to hate with hate, shame with shame, or fists with fists. He embraced the suffering, died, and conquered the shame and its trajectory of death in his resurrection. True courage. The reversal of the reversal.

And we see this, again explicitly, in John 18:19-24:

> Meanwhile, the high priest questioned Jesus about his disciples and teaching.
>
> "I have spoken openly to the world," Jesus replied. "I always taught in synagogues or at the temple, where all the Jews come together. I said nothing in secret. Why question me? Ask those who heard me. Surely they know what I said."

When Jesus said this, one of the officials nearby struck him in the face.

> "Is this the way you answer the high priest?" he demanded.
>
> "If I said something wrong," Jesus replied, "testify as to what is wrong. But if I spoke the truth, why did you strike me?" Then Annas sent him, still bound, to Caiaphas the high priest.

Annas, as one of the two high priests at the time, was likely conducting an illegal trial, given that there were no witnesses present. Jesus answered this illegality with the power to live in the light and the power to love hard questions. This wise answer revealed the ulterior agenda of Annas, and thus one of his officials "struck" Jesus in the face (in the Greek, this means with an open hand, ergo, a literal slap; but, depending on context, it can also refer to being struck, as with a rod). Jesus also challenged Annas using a different word for "strike," a stronger term. Thus, it was not a mere slap, but a strike intending to wound, as was also the case with the Sanhedrin striking Jesus with their fists at the end of the illegal trial (see Matthew 26:67-68).

So how then did Jesus fulfill his own words from the Sermon on the Mount, to turn the other cheek (cf. Lamentations 3:30)? He turned the other cheek, but challenged their basis to strike it the first time, and to see if they had the guts to strike it a second time. Jesus responded by questioning Annas, asking what it was he said that was wrong, and thus, why he was struck. Annas knew there was nothing wrong in what Jesus said, and he knew that Jesus knew that he knew that Jesus had been struck contrary to the law. Thus, Jesus challenged the illegality of the evil being done. And so he silenced his declared enemies, as Annas did not answer, but merely sent him along to Caiaphas.

Thus, to turn the other cheek, in biblical context, is a radical act of ethical and spiritual warfare, one that has the power to silence the enemies of the Gospel, and thus advance justice. And it is one that submits to the due process of law that calls for the punishment of the wrongdoer (see Romans 13:4). To turn the other cheek is an individual, not a political ethic. It is the freedom not to fear shame. Accordingly, it is an ethic that advances political persuasion for the true restraint of evil through, if necessary, imprisonment, capital punishment and just war.

Along with not physically resisting insults, Jesus then spoke of giving to those who would file lawsuit against us – giving them even more than what they want to take. Most people of the time only owned an inner garment and an outer garment. Thus, such a lawsuit to take the (outer) tunic violated Jewish law, where the cloak of a widow, and thus of any poor person, could not be taken as a pledge for some payment due, so that the person would not risk exposure to the elements (see Deuteronomy 24:17). The cloak can also symbolize inheritance.

Then Jesus spoke about going the extra mile, submitting to a category of slavery. A Roman soldier could legally compel any non-citizen to carry his pack (weighing 60 pounds on average) for a distance of one mile. Thus, to give the inner tunic as well as the outer (and become naked), and to volunteer to carry the pack a second mile, reverses the reversal. It is the power to love enemies. And in the process, it may actually shame the oppressor into relenting his evil, and/or expose its shamefulness to the power of public opprobrium, to thus "heap burning coals on his head" (words from Proverbs 25:22 and Romans 13:20).

In Romans 5:6-11, Paul assumes the power to love enemies from the Sermon on the Mount as he describes how "Christ died for the ungodly" and "when we were God's enemies, we were reconciled to him through the death of his Son." How can we, who were once enemies of the Gospel, now have anything but love for those who might still be his enemies? To do otherwise would be hypocrisy.

Love and War

How do we reconcile the power to love enemies with the Old Testament concept of "holy war?" This is where Yahweh commanded Israel, in its conquest of Canaan, to utterly destroy pagan cities, including men, women and children. Yahweh commanded the utter destruction of Israel's enemies in their war of conquest, and Jesus commands us to love our enemies.

The key is to understand, as we already noted, the overarching biblical storyline of Yahweh's preservation of the messianic lineage in the face of a pagan world where the idolatry of sorcery, sacred prostitution and child sacrifice were the trajectory of pagan religion, the devil's means to drive humanity away from their Creator.

In the Law of Moses, the messianic remnant was a political entity, protected from such pagan nations. Once Jesus came, messianic believers transcend human political boundaries and the warfare is in the heavenlies. To love human enemies is an act of war against the devil and, where we are willing, in a range of personal and political contexts, to lay our lives down for their religious, political and economic liberty to grasp who Jesus really is.

As 2 Kings 6:8-23 evidences, there is an ethical consistency between walking the extra mile, in personal ethics, and what Elisha did with the enemy Arameans, in political ethics. Elisha instructed the king of Israel not to kill the Arameans who were supernaturally captured, but to give them a feast and send them on their way. As a result, "the bands from Aram stopped raiding Israel's territory."

Here we also see the supernatural war in the heavenlies as "the chariots of fire," the warring angels of Yahweh, show up on the scene to protect Elisha. Elisha's goal was not to kill human enemies, but to exercise the power to give and the power to forgive, based on the power of informed choice rooted in the feasting ethics of *akol tokel*, and thus equaling the power to love enemies. But there are times when other enemies press the limits too far, at the devil's instigation, refuse to cease their evil, and thus merit Yahweh's judgment.

Yahweh called Abram (Abraham) to leave Babylonia, with its bloodshed, to possess some lands that were then occupied by the Amorites and other Canaanite tribes; but their measure of sin had not yet reached its fullness to merit Yahweh's judgment. But one day it would, and Abraham's descendants would be God's agents of that judgment. They would receive the land that is God's to begin with, in which Abraham had bought his burial plot, and the land would become the home for the chosen people of the messianic lineage. The capital Jerusalem, on Mount Zion, would be a "city on a hill," as a beacon of the good news in a dark world.

The four centuries of slavery, unjustly put upon the Israelites by various pharaohs, whose forefather Joseph had rescued Egypt from famine by God's revelation (and indeed, strengthened Pharaoh's power dramatically), taught the Israelites a measure of humility and dependency upon Yahweh. This was redemptively necessary, so that in being his agents of holy war against demonically governed nations, they would be as free as possible from self-aggrandizement. They would not engage in such war for the sake of plunder, and would not do so for territorial expansion against the just claims of pagan nations to their own homelands. In being Yahweh's chosen people, God told them that it was not because of their righteousness they were chosen to drive out the Canaanites. Moses makes this clear in Deuteronomy 9:4-6:

> After the LORD your God has driven them out before you, do not
> say to yourself, "The LORD has brought me here to take possession
> of this land because of my righteousness." No, it is on account of the
> wickedness of these nations that the LORD is going to drive them
> out before you. It is not because of your righteousness or your
> integrity that you are going in to take possession of their land; but on
> account of the wickedness of these nations, the LORD your God will
> drive them out before you, to accomplish what he swore to your
> fathers, to Abraham, Isaac and Jacob. Understand, then, that it is not
> because of your righteousness that the LORD your God is giving you
> this good land to possess, for you are a stiff-necked people (cf.
> Exodus 32:9; Deuteronomy 10:16; Nehemiah 9:16).

The Israelites were chosen out of Yahweh's love, and all pretense of self-justification against the pagans was removed. Yahweh credited "righteousness" to Abram – he did not earn it by human merit. The Israelites were as stubborn or stiff-necked as the pagans – just as thoroughly sinners. But they were sinners who, unlike the pagans, responded to Yahweh positively.

Yahweh said from the outset that the Amorites and other Canaanite tribes were wicked, in need of being judged. Israel was set in radical contrast to the pagan nations for whom war was a means of aggrandizement and vengeance. Israel was to exercise no vengeance as humans. They were only to serve Yahweh's vengeance, and on his terms. Their own sin was to be checked by the Law of Moses in the process, whereas pagan nations had no such law to check their sins, as they would initiate war against their enemies. As Yahweh's agents, the Israelites were to be molded into his standards, seeing the cost of sin for the demonized nations, and thus be instructed to flee idolatry themselves.

Yahweh's Patience

Yahweh demonstrates remarkable patience with sin in the Bible. The active participial nature of *moth tamuth* gives space and time for people to reap the fruit of their sins, to thus acknowledge reality and perhaps seek God in repentance, that they might be forgiven and restored (see Romans 2:4). But as well, Yahweh knows when his patience will bear fruit and when it will not, and he even goes well beyond certainty in this regard. Noah preached for 120 years, in God's timetable (see Genesis 6:3), before the Flood came, and yet no one repented. Noah was declared "a preacher of righteousness" (2 Peter 2:5).

Yahweh showed this patience with the Amorites and Canaanites, giving them 400 years to repent of their sins (see Genesis 15:12-16). Abraham's descendants would know the slavery of sin at its worst during these years,

191

and would be humbled extraordinarily before taking possession of the Promised Land. Only then could they be trusted enough to execute Yahweh's judgment on Yahweh's righteous terms, and to learn to welcome aliens into a nation where equal justice applied to all: "Do not mistreat an alien or oppress him, for you were aliens in Egypt" (Exodus 22:21; cf. Leviticus 24:22). The Amorites excelled in the triad of sorcery, sacred prostitution and child sacrifice – the ethics of the ancient serpent designed to destroy the human race, the Messiah's lineage, and thus to avert his own coming judgment.

Both Israelite and Amorite were simultaneously judged over these four centuries. The Israelites were a people who proved willing to let their stubbornness be judged and tempered by the true God and Creator. The Amorites were a people who refused to be tempered. When this season was completed, Yahweh used the Israelites as his rod of judgment, a judgment that the Canaanite tribes knowingly chose. Yahweh has great patience, but there is a limit, once people are sealed in their rebellious identities. Yahweh must judge the proxy nations of Satan's war, in order to protect the messianic lineage, in order to provide salvation for all peoples who seek the true God.

When the 400 years were complete, and Yahweh raised up Moses to be the deliverer and law giver, he was prepared to judge the wickedness of the reigning pharaoh for the history of unjustly enslaving the Israelites and making great wealth at their expense. Yahweh demonstrated great patience with the pharaoh, giving him many times to repent, but he refused.

This patience, and Yahweh's mercy being continually offered to pagan peoples in three historical contexts – the days of Noah, with the pharaoh and with the Amorites – was well known by the Israelites when they arrived at the threshold of the Promised Land.

The Conquest of Holy War

During the Exodus itself, even before the Israelites reach the Promised Land, the lineage of the ancient serpent was warring fiercely against this large group of ex-slaves who had no formal military training. In Exodus 17:8-16, at the beginning of the Exodus, the war of the ancient serpent against the messianic lineage picked up where Pharaoh left off, as the Amalekite tribe attacked Israel unprovoked. In Numbers 20:14-21, a generation later, the provocation against the Israelites in their exodus continued, as the Edomites would not let the Israelites pass through their land peaceably.

Yahweh was only giving land to the Israelites from nations that were fully demonized, who had fully and repeatedly rejected his grace. The Edomites came from Esau, Jacob's brother, and though they had their measure of sin, and were always at enmity with Israel, Yahweh still honored the integrity of their territory (see Deuteronomy 2:2-7). Thus, Israel did not provoke them even when denied an honest request.

In Numbers 21:1-3, the Canaanite king of Arad attacked the Israelites unprovoked, and the response was *haram*, the complete destruction of holy war. In Numbers 21:21ff, Israel sent messengers to Sihon, king of the Amorites, asking for permission to pass through his country, promising to touch nothing of theirs, just as promised to the king of Edom. Sihon likewise refused, and mustered his army against the Israelites; but this time, Israel fought back, completely destroyed the Amorites and occupied their land and cities, and subsequently did the same when Og, king of Bashan, attacked Israel.

In Numbers 22-25, we have the remarkable saga of Bala'am, already noted, where Israel was finally seduced into sexual immorality and sacrifices to pagan gods. For this Yahweh brought judgment through the decree of Moses, but also, upon the Midianites: "The LORD said to Moses, 'Treat the Midianites as enemies and kill them, because they treated you as enemies when they deceived you in the affair of Peor.' "

Or in other words, Yahweh was only judging those pagans who sided against the Israelites as the messianic remnant. Israel was not engaged in provocation; the devil was, behind the scenes, through these pagan peoples. Israel, after 400 years of unjust suffering, was looking for a home in which to dwell in peace. Yahweh carved out for them a modest territory of land among peoples who had already utterly exhausted his patience in their embrace of sorcery, sacred prostitution and child sacrifice. Those peoples were to be judged, and along the way, other pagan peoples not previously singled out to be judged also chose to be judged as they joined in the ancient serpent's agenda.

Thus, in Numbers 31, at the end of Moses' life, Yahweh commanded Israel to complete the vengeance upon the Midianites – even the people from whom his wife and father-in-law came. For though they were not among the pagan nations set to be judged originally, they joined those nations in opposing the messianic remnant, and brought the judgment on themselves. The cancer of their sin had to be dealt with, specifically in terms of the sexual immorality.

In Numbers 33:55-56, Moses warned the Israelites to drive out the pagans and their idols from the Promised Land.

> " 'But if you do not drive out the inhabitants of the land, those you
> allow to remain will become barbs in your eyes and thorns in your
> sides. They will give you trouble in the land where you will live.
> And then I will do to you what I plan to do with them.' "

The Canaanites had exhausted Yahweh's patience, and now they were to be judged. If they were not judged completely, then their remnants would rise again to pollute and try to kill off the messianic lineage. Psalm 106:34-

39 shows how the Israelites failed and then succumbed to idolatry and child sacrifice. Moses warned the Israelites that they must completely destroy the demonic cultures. This was "holy war."

But holy war also had stipulations on how it was to be carried out, as outlined in Deuteronomy 7:1-11. No selfish gain, no rapacity, no intermarriage with Canaanite women, no human vengeance, no nationalistic egoism, no tribalistic superiority. Rather, it was to be carried out in humility by a nation humbled by 400 years of unjust slavery, as they looked to dwell in peace in the midst of a sinful world. They were to be holy, "set apart" from all pagan influences so as to protect the messianic lineage.

Whose Side?

After the death of Moses, with the Israelites now finally done with their years in the wilderness, the book of Joshua begins with the formal conquest of Canaan. When Joshua led Israel across the Jordan, their first objective was to take the city of Jericho, a walled fortress. Rahab, the pagan prostitute who lived in the city walls, served the Israelite spies in their planning. She had heard of the reputation of Yahweh's power and goodness, and she chose to forsake her gods – and her people – in order to be reconciled to her Creator (see Joshua 2). She became an Israelite, married an Israelite, and became part of the actual messianic lineage of Jesus, being an ancestor of Boaz (who married the Moabitess Ruth), Obed, Jesse and David (see Matthew 1:5-6). She saw the goodness of Yahweh as all her pagan city did, but she alone chose the goodness for herself and her family. Had anyone else in the city wanted Yahweh's goodness instead of their idols, sorcery, sacred prostitution and child sacrifice, they too could have done likewise. Prior to the battle for the city, we read the following:

Now when Joshua was near Jericho, he looked up and saw a man standing in front of him with a drawn sword in his hand. Joshua went up to him and asked, "Are you for us or for our enemies?"

"Neither," he replied, "but as commander of the army of the LORD I have now come." Then Joshua fell face down in reverence, and asked him, "What message does my Lord have for his servant?"

The commander of the LORD's army replied, "Take off your sandals, for the place where you are standing is holy." And Joshua did so (Joshua 5:13-15).

As Joshua approached the city, an angel of God met him. Joshua asked the question of which side he was on, not yet recognizing him as an angel. The angel was the commander of Yahweh's army, not only in terms of the nation of Israel, but in the deeper reality of the spiritual warfare behind the scenes, where God's angels war on Israel's behalf against the demons who war on behalf of pagan nations, for Jesus to come as a "light to the Gentiles." The angel said he was on neither side – a powerful rebuke to any notions of self-righteousness against enemies. Rather, the implicit question for Joshua was: "Whose side are you on?"

Joshua immediately recognized this reality, humbled himself in front of the angel of God, and was told that he was standing on holy ground. It was holy because Yahweh was present with his angelic messenger, preparing for the conquest of the Promised Land. This was a holy undertaking, to be done on Yahweh's terms, not on human terms. When the angel said he was on neither side, but was serving Yahweh, he distinguished the upcoming conflict from a human one. Yahweh desires that none should perish, but with the *moth tamuth* covenantal warning of the power of informed choice, he loves the pagans enough to let them choose their own gods, but as well, they must face the consequences of their choices. Thus, Yahweh was showing his love to his enemies as he prepares them for their own chosen destruction. He loves people enough to let them choose hell, but not to impose hell on others. It was now a war of reality: Who is the true God? Yahweh Elohim of Israel or some pagan deity?

Either there is a God in heaven who made us, or else there is not. For the skeptic, if there is no God, then the contrast between the biblical self-understanding of justice, against that of all other concepts provides the greatest check against self-justification that history knows. But if there is a God in heaven who judges the deeds of men, then we need to be aware of the judgment we will face when life is done. If Yahweh is no god, then all peoples can go to war as they see fit. If Yahweh is the true God, then what we have in the holy war of Israel against the pagan nations is a matter of justice for the sake of inviting all people to choose salvation. It is the power of informed of choice, the fairness of reaping what we sow.

People who have suffered evil want justice. And if there is no justice exacted upon wicked people and nations, then evil metastasizes. According to the power of informed choice, we all reap what we sow in the course of human events. As well, Yahweh intervenes and makes specific judgments. The question becomes this: Who alone can judge justly, and can any fault be lodged against Yahweh? Against the One who defines the power to give and the power to forgive, but necessarily is consistent with the power of informed choice where people who love darkness will receive what they have loved? As image-bearers of God, as the covenant people descended from Abraham, the Israelites were chosen to be God's agents of holy judgment against a people who were completely evil, a people who as proxies of the ancient serpent wanted to destroy the Messiah's coming, to destroy his goodness. And only Yahweh Elohim could decree such a judgment which is truly just and ethically loving at the same time – giving all people what and whom they have loved.

What followed was the Israelite campaign to take the Promised Land. Beginning with Jericho in Joshua 6, it was a spiritual contest between the Ark of the Covenant and the pagan deities of a city, a city that knew of Yahweh's deliverance of the Israelites from Egyptian captivity but had no interest, with the exception of Rahab and her household. Yahweh supernaturally intervened and the city walls fell. Joshua commanded his army to destroy all living creatures in the city – people and animals. The Hebrew word for destroy in this context is *haram*, which means a specific type of destruction that is devoted to Yahweh. In other words, the devotion to false gods and the power of demons was being destroyed, and replaced by a devotion to the true God. No human ego of conquest.

The nation of Israel was Yahweh's agency of executing judgment, and only insofar as they depended on his supernatural oversight as their King. God knows that the children were innocent in the sense of not being old enough yet to judge between good and evil – and in his judgment he will judge accordingly. But he also knows that any survivors of a pagan culture would likely return to their origins, that such children would grow up and do the same as their parents apart from a culture-wide redemptive success. The very possibility of seduction must be removed to ensure protection. It was ensured with the conversion of Rahab's household, because they chose to convert. She was the exception that proved the rule. But the rest of Jericho's households chose to cling to their gods and evil practices. And households had an integral unity of belief and identity that our modern individualism has largely put aside.

This is part of the corporate responsibility that individuals and nations hold together. If a tyrant arises in their midst, the people are responsible for it to the degree that they do not resist tyranny according to their abilities. If a whole people resist a tyrant at the risk of their lives, even if a modest portion of the people resist, the tyrant cannot continue. The tyrant needs a large level of complicity, a) among the elitists in their cooperation however they are to be paid off, and then b) among the people by their fear to challenge the tyrant with his elitists, who thus provide his necessary economic base. Accordingly, even people who live under totalitarian regimes have moral culpabilities in terms of the evil conducted by their tyrants.

These ethics of holy war, again, started with judgment on Israel. Because Achan disobeyed the stipulations and stole valuables in the conquest of Jericho, he suffered the capital punishment as he was warned (see Joshua 7). Where else has this ethic of judging yourself first before judging others ever existed in military ethics prior to and apart from the Bible?

As Israel took Jericho, then Ai, we also see the biblical balance between sovereignty and choice. Yahweh intervened, yet Israel participated fully in the process. We do not have a tyrannical god who fatalistically pulls the strings of people as puppets, nor do we have people as their own gods who alone can save themselves. Yahweh's sovereignty provides for human freedom, and the balance produces the humility of worship, and the diligence of responsible action.

Amalekite Evil

In Deuteronomy 25:17-19, in reference to Exodus 17:8-16, Moses reminds Israel how the Amalekites had attacked Israel when they were leaving Egypt: "When you were weary and worn out, they met you on your journey and cut off all who were lagging behind."

What the Amalekites did to Israel was central in the nation's memory, and Moses was emphatic in calling the Israelites to remember it, and to fulfill Yahweh's call to wipe them out completely. The apostle Peter says: "Your enemy the devil prowls around like a roaring lion looking for someone to devour" (1 Peter 5:8). The solitary lion, hunting for prey, will not attack a herd of cape buffalos head on. This is how the Amalekites attacked Israel unprovoked. Not a military clash, but an attempt at genocide.

Finally, the Amalekites were judged at Yahweh's instructions to King Saul. But Saul did not fully carry out Yahweh's instructions, seeking human glory and plunder from the conquest. Thus Samuel had to finish the job, and Saul was judged too (see 1 Samuel 15; cf. David's additional role in 1 Samuel 30).

The Amalekites and the Great Commission?

Yahweh gave Saul a mission to wipe out the cancer of the Amalekite culture. What mission do we have today as Christians? It is the Great Commission that Jesus gave his disciples after his resurrection – to go into the whole world with the message of the good news (Matthew 28:16-20). Its instruction is to give to those who would take from us, to bless those who would curse us, to love those who would hate us. The messianic line, from Abraham, was ordained to bless all nations (see Genesis 12:1-3); yet, blessings act in concert with the power of informed choice, namely, those who curse the blessings end up bringing curses upon themselves. They do not want the messianic blessings, so God gives them what they choose.

What, therefore, is the consistency between the mission to destroy the Amalekites and the Great Commission? They are consistent in that the Bible understands the demonic nature behind the pagan religions and the nations seeking to wipe out the messianic lineage. There could be no Great Commission apart from the preservation of theocratic Israel, and the understandings of the Law of Moses, which Jesus came to fulfill.

The love God has for us, as those who were once his enemies, requires the separation between temporal and eternal enemies. Temporal enemies are loved until they seal their choices in eternity and become eternal self-chosen enemies of God, and even the love continues in the sense that they have been given their choice. But as Satan rebelled against Yahweh, along with other rebellious angels, and they are our only true enemies, so the demonized cultures of the various Canaanite nations were the locus for the devil's eternal enemy status against Israel.

Just as Rahab had the freedom to escape judgment in choosing to flee a wicked culture, so too, throughout the Old Testament, Yahweh was always patient with pagan nations, until or unless they reached a point of truly seared consciences where they stubbornly became committed to the destruction of the messianic seed, even if it cost them their own lives. The power to love enemies is present throughout the Old Testament (e.g., Deuteronomy 23:7-8; 2 Kings 6:8-23; Proverbs 25:21-22). The Lord did that wherever possible, but he also preserved the Messiah's covenant community, before and after his coming. As well, in the book of Jonah, the prophet's very mission to the Ninevites was predicated on Yahweh's power to love enemies – a lesson Jonah was reticent to learn. He spoke of how "Those who cling to worthless idols forfeit the grace that could be theirs" (2:8). In other words, the power to love enemies was recognized in desiring grace to be chosen instead of worthless idols.

With this understood, we must be as ruthless with sin in our lives as Yahweh is with the devil. Cut it out completely, lest it pollute and eventually take us down. Yahweh has always shown love to his enemies throughout Scripture, but there is a limit to his willingness to let them pollute the lives of others. We are called to show love to our enemies today, and part of that love involves the preaching of repentance and the judgment that is to come.

The real war now is where we war against the devil and his demons through the power of prayer, to remove their influence from the lives of peoples and nations. God loves us enough to let us choose hell, and he never coerces us into life or death. This is why the biblical power of informed choice is the hermeneutic for judging the Bible's consistency in how God treats us – friend and foe alike, the same standard applies. Judgment upon Amalekite evil and the Great Commission are part of the same storyline. God desires all people to be saved (e.g., 1 Timothy 2:4), but will not force them.

Yahweh's Judgment of the Chosen People by Means of Pagan Nations

Various skeptics take umbrage that the Israelites would judge other nations in the act of holy war. Of course, skeptics believe this is a self-assigned role of the Israelites, the "Chosen People," but even yet, they abhor the concept of a God who would do so. In the purpose and history of holy war according to the Bible, tracing back to the original authority that Adam should have exercised over the ancient serpent, it was defensive in nature against the devil and his pagan nations. Yahweh called for the Israelites to engage in only one offensive war ever, to claim the Promised Land after their exodus from slavery. It sought to preserve the messianic lineage of the One who was to come and save all mankind. It put severe restrictions on the Israelites that are very un-self serving, which no pagan or secular nation ever has placed upon itself.

In chapter five, we saw how the book of Habakkuk revolves around one theme – namely, that Yahweh used pagan nations to punish the sins of the Jews. He held the Israelites and Jews to a higher standard as his covenantal people, and when they forfeited the covenant, Yahweh used pagan nations to judge them – in particular the Assyrians in 722-21 B.C. and the

Babylonians in 605-586 B.C. Yahweh had promised repeatedly in the Law of Moses that such judgment would come (e.g., Deuteronomy 8:19-20; 28:15-68). Or to put it another way, the land itself would vomit the Israelites out, as it had vomited out the pagans beforehand (see Leviticus 18:24-28). Thus, here is a complete equanimity in both judgment and mercy, and where God "shows no favoritism" (Romans 2:11). The power of informed choice is consistent throughout the Bible, and all "men are without excuse" (Romans 1:20) if they refuse God's fully demonstrable goodness.

The Imprecatory Psalms

Another place where skeptics have questioned the fairness of God toward the enemies of Israel is in what is known as the "imprecatory psalms," where curses are pronounced, or "called down" from above, that is, from God. An imprecation, by definition, cannot come from human will, but by divine will only, from "above" the human will.

At the conclusion of Psalm 137, we read:

Remember O LORD, what the Edomites did

on the day Jerusalem fell.

"Tear it down," they cried,

"tear it down to its foundations!"

O Daughter of Babylon, doomed to destruction,

happy is he who repays you

for what you have done to us –

he who seizes your infants

and dashes them against the rocks (vv. 7-9).

At the end of Psalm 139, where David has been celebrating the presence of Yahweh, from which he cannot flee, the focus abruptly changes in another representation of the imprecatory genre:

If only you would slay the wicked, O God!

Away from me, you bloodthirsty men!

They speak of you with evil intent;

your adversaries misuse your name.

Do I not hate those who hate you, O LORD,

and abhor those who rise up against you?

I have nothing but hatred for them;

I count them my enemies.

Search me, O God, and know my heart;

test me and know my anxious thoughts.

See if there is any offensive way in me,

and lead me in the way everlasting (vv. 19-24).

With a foundation in place that includes a grasp of the power of informed choice in service to the messianic lineage, it is straightforward to understand Psalm 137. The Jews were under the judgment of Yahweh as they lost the city and the temple, and were therefore exiled to Babylon. All their joy was removed, yet their captors tormented them, not dissimilar to the horror of the Nazis coercing Jewish musicians to play for them in the concentration camps.

In response, the psalmist gives the expression of the exiled Jews – that to sing the songs of Yahweh in a foreign land was the same as forgetting their homeland, and this they would never do. They spoke a self-maledictory curse consistent with covenantal law – that the loss of employment (skill of the "right hand"), and death by starvation in a siege (the "tongue cling[ing] to the roof of [the] mouth"), as many of their brethren had already suffered – would be superior to forgetting Jerusalem. In their pain at the dawning realization of the covenantal stipulations landing on them for their rebellion, they cried out to Yahweh for justice against their enemies. The Edomites, descendants of Esau, and always warring against the Israelites, were cheerleaders for the Babylonians. They egged them on, calling for the complete destruction of the city's walls and foundations.

In response, the psalmist cries out to Yahweh to remember their sin. But there were no more specifics called for than that. Let the Edomites reap what they have sown, but how that happens was left in the hands of the true Judge. There was no humanly taken vengeance expressed toward the Edomites, where they wished more than equal justice, which they completely trust into Yahweh's hands. Vengeance belongs only to Yahweh. The Jews were reaping what they have sown, and did not sit as self-appointed judges over the Edomites.

Then the psalmist prophesies the destruction of Babylon, as other prophets have already done. He speaks of the "happiness" of those (the Medes) who will carry out the destruction of Babylon. And he does so with the same specificity by which Isaiah says that the Medes will do this to the Babylonians, as the final destiny of Babylon will be like Sodom and Gomorrah (see Isaiah 13, especially vv. 15-22). Isaiah speaks of the Medes treating Babylon the way Babylon treated Jerusalem, as Yahweh chooses to use the Medes as his rod of judgment.

During the siege of Jerusalem, there was great suffering with the starvation, disease and a descent into cannibalism that resulted. Once the wall was breached and the Babylonian army poured in, the Babylonians were ruthless with those still in the city and those who had just fled. Part of this included their demonic happiness at grabbing an infant out of the mother's arms, and dashing the child against the rocks in her presence. She had to watch the fruit of her womb, the one she had nursed, become splattered blood and entrails as she screamed in horror, before the sword was turned on her.

The psalmist declares in the face of this that the judgment of Yahweh, the *moth tamuth* of the power of informed choice, will also visit the Babylonians in the same fashion. Judgment will come, but Yahweh is the Accountant and the Judge, not Judah. As Babylon's soldiers had sinful glee in their killing of the Jews, so too would the Medes have sinful glee when they dashed Babylonian infants against the rocks. But the Jews will not participate in such revenge or sinful glee – the psalmist merely prophesied the quid pro quo *moth tamuth* reality between the Medes and Babylonians.

When we look at the restrictions placed on Israel in the few times the nation was commanded to execute holy war, we see the opposite of such glee. We see a former nation of slaves doing Yahweh's work consistent with the power of informed of choice, which the pagan nations were aware of through Noah, and as Paul speaks of in Romans 1. Even yet, Israel failed many times to complete it as Psalm 106 details. Their instincts, molded by the Exodus and Law of Moses, were the opposite of the territorial expansionism of pagan nations who served gods of destruction.

Only Genesis 1-2 has a positive view of God's nature, and in him we see the power to give. There is no destruction in Yahweh's character in the order of creation; and in the reversal of the reversal, Yahweh only destroys destruction, and always in a fashion consistent with the power of informed choice. And this is exactly what the writer of Psalm 137 proclaims.

The conclusion of Psalm 139 is in the same vein as Psalm 137. The psalm's overall theme is beautiful in portraying the omnipresence of Yahweh – that he is present with David everywhere, no matter how alienated his circumstance might be. In this context, toward the end of the psalm, and as the one who also wrote Psalm 22, which Jesus quoted on the cross in the presence of his enemies, David calls on Yahweh to slay his enemies, to slay those who are in the devil's service to kill the messianic lineage.

He "hates" those who hate Yahweh. Why? Because he loves the Lord, and his hatred was inflamed by those who blasphemed Yahweh's name, who were ultimately in service to the eternal enemy. Yahweh loved Lucifer enough to allow him to rebel, become the devil, and thus choose his own destiny. In human emotions, hatred can represent the flip side of love when a betrayal of a loved one is sealed in finality. The power to love enemies in biblical ethics is purposed to redeem God's enemies, but if they refuse, the love continues in that Yahweh respects their power of informed choice, which is his universal gift. They were as free to say no as they were to say yes. It is love that defines hate ("God is Love" in 1 John 4:8); just as it is light that defines darkness ("God is light" in 1 John 1:5).

David was so confident in this biblical balance that he concluded the psalm the way he started it, with an appeal to have Yahweh search his heart and discern if there were any offensive ways in him. Thus, his "hatred" of Yahweh's enemies is not offensive, by necessary inference. This final verse is beautiful and often quoted in the church. But how often do we see it quoted in the context of the preceding verse? It is a matter of integrity.

Rejoicing in Judgment

It is also important to understand the context of theocratic Israel. David was not talking about personal ethics, but about the ethics of war, where he was dealing with nations who were sworn enemies to the messianic lineage. These same ethics are evident in the Song of Moses in Exodus 15:1-21. After the deliverance from 400 years of cruel slavery into the temporal Promised Land, the Israelites were overjoyed at their salvation, that "The horse and its rider he has hurled into the sea," that the enemy is "shattered" and "consumed like stubble," for the enemy had "boasted" about gorging themselves on the destruction of the Israelites. This is the war of the ancient serpent against the remnant of the messianic lineage.

Then in Revelation 18:1-19:3, there is celebration over the destruction of "Babylon the Great," in a genre that reflects the imprecatory psalms. The nation of Babylon no longer exists at this time, and John is using it as a figure for a spiritual wickedness at work in present and future political context. It is a haunt for every foul demon, as a metaphor for the congregation of the demonic who are Yahweh's enemies, along with those who choose to reside there with Satan as their god.

The heavenly chorus rejoices over the judgment of Babylon the great prostitute, because she has polluted the world and shed the blood of God's people. In this rejoicing, there is no human retribution. A fully redeemed person will never have joy in the intrinsic nature of retribution, of the wicked suffering in their chosen home of hell, just as Yahweh takes no pleasure in the death of the wicked (see Ezekiel 18:23). Rather what we have here in Revelation 18 is the joy of salvation – for the saints being delivered once and for all from the wickedness of the ancient serpent and his false kingdom.

For those of us who have experienced even a small portion of the evil that the Bible judges the devil for, we know how it wears out the body and soul. And when deliverance comes from evil, we too rejoice, and are glad for Yahweh's judgment upon it. God is true and just in all his judgments, whereas all the false gods are false and unjust. We are given the freedom to choose in whom to believe. Thus, in *Handel's Messiah*, the *Hallelujah Chorus*, which is taken from Revelation 18, follows on the heels of singing from the imprecatory Psalm 2 where the Messiah dashes his enemies to pieces like pottery.

The Power to Love Enemies

The power to love enemies is powerful, and not facile. It is the height of the Sermon on the Mount, and yet it is muscular at the same time in terms of spiritual warfare. For the sake of showing God's love to all who would accept it, especially those who are currently his enemies, we must a) fight the devil in the heavenlies by the power of the Holy Spirit, and b) be willing to lay our lives down for others, just as a soldier does in a just war. This is a risk-taking love, knowing that we who are believers were once enemies of the Gospel in our unbelief. But then Jesus suffered, died and rose again, and now we are reconciled to him, able to share that reconciliation with all people.

♦ ♦ ♦

Chapter Six
The Power to Forgive

So Simple, It Seems

When I originally grasped these pillars, I only had five in mind – the power to love enemies was subsumed under the power to forgive. But as I thought and prayed about it more, I saw the need to make a distinction, and hence, six pillars. Since then, these six have proved satisfactory in summing up the Bible ethically. The final two pillars – the power to love enemies and the power to forgive – equal two redemptive ethics that aim at a restoration of the four pillars in the order of creation.

Due to politics or culture or tribal history, there are many people who may consider themselves our enemies, not because they know us personally, but because they find themselves in a "camp" which is ideologically opposed to our "camp." This is one matter when it comes to learning to love and forgive.

But it is entirely a different matter when it comes to someone close to us. The power to forgive is so simple, it seems, but yet it can be the most difficult. It is not a matter of intellectual grasp, but of the will and emotions.

Thus, in many instances, it is emotionally easier to love someone who is an enemy, than to forgive a friend. Unforgiveness is most often the state of affairs between two people who are, or once were, friends, and especially in the case of relations between husband and wife, parents and children, or siblings.

In chapter 3 we spoke of the power of bitterness and how it can be defined as "trust betrayed," which, if allowed to grow, only deadens the human spirit. Unforgiveness is deathly in its impact in terms of heart, soul, mind and strength. It shrinks humanity relentlessly until given up in favor of the power to forgive. Unless the power to forgive is radically embraced, beginning in the marriage relationship where the power to give originates in human society, this downward cycle of sin's vortex more perversely justifies itself and destroys individuals, families and nations.

All people need forgiveness, and all but the most hardened of heart yearn for it. But where is the power to accomplish it? It ultimately comes down to the foundation of:

creation → sin → redemption.

Or we can sum up the six pillars this way:

the power to give → the rejection of the gift → the power to
forgive.

In other words, in the biblical order of creation, Yahweh Elohim gives us all his blessings, we choose to reject his terms and go our own way, yet his power to give remains his nature. The power to forgive equals the final restoration of the power to give in Jesus. Or to put it another way, the power to give and the power to forgive equal the bookends of the Bible – God gives, we blow it, and he forgives. Eight words that sum up Biblical Theology 101.

Thus, in the face of sin and suffering, the power to give becomes the power to forgive. To forgive is to give in the face of broken trust, so as to restore us to the simplicity of an unpolluted power to give and receive.

In Jeremiah 31:33-34, as the new covenant is promised, we read these words:

"This is the covenant I will make with the house of Israel after that time," declares the LORD. "I will put my law in their minds and write it on their hearts. I will be their God, and they will be my people.

"No longer will a man teach his neighbor, or a man his brother, saying, 'Know the LORD,' because they will all know me, from the least of them to the greatest," declares the LORD. "For I will forgive their wickedness and will remember their sins no more."

The Hebrew word in play for "remember" is *zakar*. It means that our sins will be remembered no more, not in the sense of a loss of memory on Yahweh's part, but in terms of an accounting ledger. The record of our sins is destroyed, and we become a free people, with no more debt to the sins of our past.

A Very Short Sermon

Quite some years ago I read a story, or heard it told, by South American evangelist Juan Carlos Ortiz, concerning a Brazilian pastor of a large Pentecostal church. (I hope it is not apocryphal, as I remember it clearly – it sure is good). The pastor was frustrated with an outward and dead religiosity in his church, despite some energy in worship. One Sunday, when it came time to preach, he stood up and simply stated the essence of John 13:34-35 in three words: "Love one another." Then he sat down, and asked the choir to sing the closing hymn.

People were astonished, yet it was the buzz for the next week. With people's eager anticipation, and many more in attendance, the pastor stood up the next Sunday and again said, "Love one another." The buzz became a roar, and the church was packed even more the third week. And the sermon? Everyone already had it memorized: "Love one another."

Then the sermon began to sink in, and people started loving one another, as they never had – in tangible and transforming ways. True revival. This was "a word in season," and likely not replicable in the exact details, but oh so powerful in its simplicity.

Likewise a three-word sermon could be preached, in season, "Forgive one another" (with Colossians 3:13 as the text).

Out of the Depths

The biblical storyline shows the downward spiral of sin, the betrayals of trust once embraced in the Garden, and ultimately the human impossibility of climbing out. In view of this trajectory, the apostle Paul speaks of the Law of Moses as a tutor or custodian of the faith, until the Messiah was revealed.

At crucial places we see how the Bible and its storyline chronicle the extraordinary depths of broken trust, and how even the most godly of people could not fully realize the power to forgive, though there were glimmers. Most of us know the outline of these stories, and their cumulative effect drives home the need for the power to forgive. But a work was waiting to be accomplished, one that would clothe us with such power.

Abel offered his best in his sacrifice to Yahweh, but Cain gave no more than a passive nod to the goodness of Yahweh. So in jealously, Cain murdered his brother, and instead of seeking forgiveness, he condemned himself as a wanderer. He was more satisfied in owning his self-justifying bitterness, than in reconciliation. Cain's descendant Lamech heightened this reversal as he boasted in his bigamy and murder.

Wickedness spread through the following generations, and the lineage of Cain – that of the ancient offspring now – triumphed over all but one man, Noah, and his family. So Yahweh purged the planet, which cannot purge the human heart, and broken trust was quick to reassert itself in the matter of Ham against Noah. Then in subsequent generations, the Tower of Babel was built and became the foundation of pagan religion. It was a complete rejection of Yahweh and gloried in a self-asserting pride.

Pride never wants to admit the need for forgiveness. So the idolatry, debauchery and killings continued.

Abraham was then the remnant who worshiped Yahweh Elohim as the one true God, who received the great promise that through his seed all nations would be blessed. Yet he faltered in the matter of Hagar, and this set up the war between Sarah and Hagar, between Ishmael and Isaac, which traces to this day in the ceaseless turmoil of the Middle East and beyond. Imagine the pain between the two brothers, reaping the fruit of choices that preceded them.

We see the horror of Sodom and Gomorrah, where the idea of forgiveness was completely foreign, even as Abraham interceded in prayer for them.

Then we see the war in the womb and across the subsequent years between Jacob and Esau – betrayals in many directions, attempts at reconciliation – yet their descendants were always at war with each other. Then the betrayal of Joseph by his brothers, yet he rescued them and his father, Jacob (Israel), in the end, extending great forgiveness, only to have a subsequent pharaoh betray the Israelites. They were a humbled people as Moses led them in the exodus to Canaan, and gave than the very Law written in stone by the finger of God.

But after Joshua, many of the judges descended into self-serving purposes, rejecting Yahweh as their true King, pitting the final Israelite judge, Samuel, against the first and completely self-serving king, Saul. Yahweh redeemed the pagan styled kingship with David, yet David committed a treacherous act of adultery and conspiracy to commit murder, and in Psalm 51 we read David's heart-cry for forgiveness. This cry was something Saul never considered for his own sins. And throughout the psalms, David and others often lament their rejections, the enemies that surround him, and their thirsting for forgiveness and redemption.

When, due to his folly of multiple marriages where he did not reverse this pagan element of Saul's kingship, David set up the competition and jealousies between sons of different mothers. One son, Amnon, raped his half-sister Tamar, David was furious, but also impotent to intervene due to different mothers. Tamar's full brother Absalom bid his time and then murdered Amnon in revenge, and the cycle of revenge ramped up, precluding the power to forgive.

And onward through the end of Israel and Judah, the destruction of Jerusalem and the temple, and 400 years waiting for the Messiah between Malachi and John the Baptist.

The Centrality of Forgiveness

When Jesus came, his Sermon on the Mount summed up what the Law requires of us in the heart, and which we cannot fulfill apart from God's grace. After Jesus taught on the power to love enemies, he moved into charity, prayer and fasting, and linked them all together. Then came the Lord's Prayer and its trajectory of the power to forgive (my translation):

> Our Father in heaven, holy is your name.
>
> Your kingdom come, your will be done on earth as it is in
>
> heaven.
>
> Give us today our daily bread, and forgive us our debts, as
>
> we forgive our debtors.
>
> And do not bring us into temptation, but deliver us from the
>
> evil one (Matthew 6:9-13).

These four lines are comprehensive in addressing the arenas of family, politics, economics and spiritual warfare. But for here, we can note the inclusive trajectory of the prayer with Jesus' subsequent words to his disciples:

> For if you forgive men when they sin against you, your heavenly Father will also forgive you. But if you do not forgive men their sins, your Father will not forgive your sins" (Matthew 6:14-15).

Jesus is clear. Unless we forgive those who sin against us, we ourselves will not be forgiven. Eternal life hangs in the balance. Once, when teaching the Lord's Prayer as part of a seminar in California, a woman asked me if this means that people who do not forgive others will not enter heaven. My answer was to look at the words of Jesus – they speak for themselves. Heaven is the community of the forgiving and forgiven; hell is the hole of unforgiveness and bitterness.

All the concerns that Jesus raises in the Lord's Prayer about God's will and its accomplishment, the provision for our daily needs, forgiveness of debts, and deliverance from the evil one, are then encapsulated in the sentence that follows its recitation: "For if you forgive..." The "if" clause is in place because the question of forgiveness is central. The power to forgive opens up the revelation of God's will, the provision of our needs, and spiritual authority over the devil. It is so simple and yet so difficult, and I think we all know it. It is a matter of the will, and whether or not we will accept the power of informed choice and choose unilaterally to forgive those who have sinned against us, as God in Christ unilaterally extended forgiveness to us.

In Luke 5:17-26, we read how Jesus placed the need for forgiveness ahead of the power to heal. Some friends of a paralytic man brought him to Jesus, and Jesus declared the man was forgiven of his sins. Some Pharisees and teachers of the law present were incensed at Jesus for assuming God's prerogative to forgive. So to give evidence of his authority to forgive sins, Jesus healed the man.

All demonstrations of signs and wonders by Jesus and the apostles were a taste of the power of the age to come, of the resurrection body, but unattainable apart from forgiveness.

A little later in Luke, in the context of material from the Sermon on the Mount, Jesus says simply: "Forgive and you will be forgiven. Give and it will be given to you" (6:37). In other words, starting with his redemptive mission, Jesus gives us the bookends of the Bible in two short sentences – the essence of the six pillars of biblical power.

The Enjoyment of Bitterness?

Many times when preaching or teaching on this subject, I have asked the audience if anyone there has ever experienced bitterness. And of course, there is a near universal affirmation – and a few chuckles as well.

Then I give a simple two-word definition of bitterness, "trust betrayed," as referenced earlier. Namely, it is not the pain from some distant enemy, but from someone we deeply trusted, a vulnerability exposed and trampled; from a husband or wife, parent or sibling, roommate or business partner, et al. Then I ask if anyone has ever plotted revenge, and the smiles and chuckles grow more. We all know that vengeance belongs to the Lord, but yet, how many of us have nonetheless plotted revenge, even if never acted on?

There are two ways to accomplish vengeance, as I mentioned in chapter 3 – the pagan way and the "sanctified" way. In the former, we merely push the person in front of an oncoming Mack truck. In the latter, we pray that the person will trip and fall in front of the oncoming Mack truck.

But if we are wise, we will eschew these feelings as soon as possible. I remember once as a teenager, in the laundry room in our basement, wrestling with bitterness. Then it hit me so clear – it was a downward spiral, and either I could yield to its idolatry and be sucked into an unending cycle set on fire by hell, or by faith in Jesus, I could repent of the bitterness and be rescued. The more we wallow in bitterness, like quicksand, the more we distance ourselves from the possibility of the freedom of forgiveness. Bitterness is idolatry because we place ourselves ahead of God's prerogative for justice and mercy. When we are bitter, we play God. And when we are bitter, we are incapable of forgiveness. If we wrestle with bitterness, then we need to grasp Jesus on the cross.

The Greatest Power Contest in History

In these pages we have spoken of power, and it is in the work of the cross where the power to forgive is demonstrated, and purchased on our behalf. This is the greatest power contest in history – and perhaps the greatest place of awe-inspiring Christian doctrine. It is where Jesus, falsely accused and betrayed, crid out on the cross, "Father, forgive them, for they do not know what they are doing" (Luke 23:34).

In Genesis 3:15, Yahweh Elohim prophesied that the seed of the woman, the Messiah, would crush the head (authority) of the ancient serpent (in the atoning death, resurrection and Second Coming), but that the serpent would first strike his heel (seeking to cause his death on the cross). It is the power to give and the power to forgive versus the power to take and destroy.

Jesus, in his greatest weakness, proves infinitely superior to Satan's greatest self-aggrandizement. It was the weakness of the woman's womb, suffering under the curse brought on by the serpent that gives birth to the One who curses the curse (see Col. 2:13-15) and restores the promises of the order of creation.

Matthew 26:36-44 reads:

Then Jesus went with his disciples to a place called Gethsemane, and he said to them, "Sit here while I go over there and pray." He

218

took Peter and the two sons of Zebedee along with him, and he began to be sorrowful and troubled. Then he said to them, "My soul is overwhelmed with sorrow to the point of death. Stay here and keep watch with me."

Going a little further, he fell with his face to the ground and prayed, "My Father, if it is possible, may this cup be taken from me. Yet not as I will, but as you will."

Then he returned to his disciples and found them sleeping. "Could you men not keep watch with me for one hour?" he asked Peter. "Watch and pray so that you will not fall into temptation. The spirit is willing, but the body is weak."

He went away a second time and prayed, "My Father, if it is not possible for this cup to be taken away unless I drink it, may your will be done."

When he came back, he again found them sleeping, because their eyes were heavy. So he left them and went away once more and prayed the third time, saying the same thing.

In the Garden of Gethsemane, the devil was returning for the "opportune time" he had sought since the temptation in the wilderness (see Luke 4:13). He was seeking to kill Jesus, and Judas had already been recruited as his chief "offspring" to betray him to the authorities (see Matthew 26:20-25; John 13:21-30).

In Gethsemane, the hour was spiritually heavy and dark, Jesus knew it, and the disciples were overwhelmed by it in their confusion. The devil was bringing his greatest strength against their greatest moment of weakness, to get them to succumb to temptation, flee and deny their Lord. Jesus knew he was to become the Lamb of God, take onto his body the sins of all human history to pay the penalty of death in our stead, and to suffer the abuse of the ancient serpent in the process. He knew he was about to expose his greatest weakness to the onslaught of the devil's greatest strength of hatred.

It is remarkable to consider. When we think of all the wars, famines, floods, fires, storms, deaths, divorces, rapes, abortions, betrayals, accidents, sexually transmitted diseases, shattered hopes, leprosies, gangrenes, leukemias and cancers – when we think of all the pains suffered by the billions of people that have lived from Adam to the present, and to the day when Christ returns – all this is laid onto Jesus' body on the cross, at one moment in time which uniquely intersected with eternity. Jesus groaned deeply as he considered his destiny, and in anguish he prayed so earnestly that sweat like drops of blood fell to the ground (see Luke 22:44). He had to do it alone, as his disciples fell asleep in this hour of trial.

We also see the power of informed choice at play. In knowing the cup of suffering he had to drink, Jesus was free, in triune community, to ask the Father if the cup could be taken away from him – if there were another way. In his humanity as the Son of Man, he did not want to suffer; in his deity as the Son of God, he knew he had to. There was no other way but to suffer and die so that Adam's race could be redeemed. In other words, the Son of God fully chose to die for us, even in the face of his humanity.

This reality is all the more compelling when we consider how Jesus was utterly abandoned on the cross by God the Father, and as he suffered for our sins, he gave up all his power of deity (see Matthew 27:32-51).

In Philippians 2:5-11, we read Paul's poem that theologically sums up what was happening in the crucifixion:

Your attitude should be the same as that of Christ Jesus:

Who, being in very nature God,

did not consider equality with God something to be grasped,

but made himself nothing,

taking the very nature of a servant,

being made in human likeness.

And being found in appearance as a man,

he humbled himself

and became obedient to death – even death on a cross!

Therefore God exalted him to the highest place

and gave him the name that is above every name,

that at the name of Jesus every knee should bow,

in heaven and on earth and under the earth,

and every tongue should confess that Jesus Christ is Lord,

to the glory of God the Father.

The power contest was between the integrity of Jesus as the Son of God, in whom all divine power resides; and the devil, in whom there was no integrity, and in whom there was no power apart from the pretense he used to deceive people into thinking he had any real power and authority to begin with. To demonstrate this truth, to slay the falsehood of dualism, Jesus willingly laid aside all his divine power, and placed himself wholly in the clutches of the devil's supposed power.

I do not believe the devil understood the nature of the atonement Jesus was accomplishing, nor especially the resurrection to follow, just as the prologue to John's gospel says – the darkness cannot understand or overcome the light. Rather, like a cornered snake, the devil simply struck out irrationally against his enemy. He simply wanted to fight against God any way he could manage. Here the serpent was striking at Jesus' authority and the goodness of God.

In Matthew 27:43, the chief priests quoted a phrase from Psalm 22:8, "He trusts in God" (Yahweh). This is from a messianic psalm that lays out great detail concerning the events of the crucifixion, and the chief priests were likewise unaware how in their rebellion they were still in service to Yahweh's sovereignty, quoting from a psalm Jesus was fulfilling that very moment. Jesus was trusting in God, trusting him enough to die for our sins, and to forgive the hatred and ignorance of those who were crucifying and mocking him.

Jesus thus refused to use his power of deity and come off the cross. He put aside his equality with God at this point, and as Philippians 2:8 states it, he became a servant who humbled himself to obedience in the face of death on the cross. Earlier, too, he refused such power as he aimed for the cross.

As well, when Jesus was arrested, one of the disciples drew a sword and struck the servant of the high priest, cutting off his ear. Jesus commanded the man to put his sword away (after he healed the slave's ear in Luke 22:51). Then he said, "Do you think I cannot call on my Father, and he will at once put at my disposal twelve legions of angels? But how then would the Scriptures be fulfilled that say it must happen this way?" (Matthew 26:53-54).

A full Roman legion equaled 6,000 soldiers. Jesus was saying he could snap his fingers and have 72,000 warring angels of God at his disposal. It would be no contest, if Jesus chose to meet the devil on these terms. But to do so would violate the power of informed choice and the gift of the image of God.

Jesus was reversing the reversal and refusing reliance on the power of the sword, or on divine military power. That military power will come with his second coming, when Jesus returns with an angelic army. That will be a military power against those who have refused such goodness, after the reversal of the reversal has availed every living person of the power to choose life.

Yahweh could have earlier marched into the Garden of Eden with 72,000 of the faithful angels, had he wished to put an end to the devil's rebellion, then and there. But then we could never have been redeemed. We had to face the curse of *moth tamuth*, and Jesus had to pay that price of death at just the right time. Yahweh promised Adam and Eve that they would reap what they had sown, because they were not animals or puppets. So God maintained the power of informed choice in the face of the serpent having kidnapped his offspring, seeking to turn them into puppets.

The Power of Being Forsaken

As the power conflict escalated, and darkness now covered the earth for three hours in the middle of the day, Jesus cried out the opening words of Psalm 22:1: "My God, my God, why have you forsaken me?" Those standing by, being ignorant of what was happening, confused Jesus' cry, spoken in Aramaic, as though he were calling for Elijah (similar sounding – and Elijah was one who had not tasted death). They reflected a common superstition, which held that Elijah would come down and help a person in distress if called upon. And they waited to see if this "Elijah" would appear. But to any biblically literate Jew who might have been nearby, like the faithful women disciples who were there, it would have been recognized, if not fully understood as to why, that Jesus was quoting this central messianic psalm.

Psalm 22, as we noted earlier, is a psalm in which David shows the anguish of being surrounded by his enemies, and being completely abandoned to their wickedness. It expresses astonishing details that are also uniquely met in the factors surrounding Jesus' crucifixion. As David cried out in anguish at the hatred of his enemies as they devoured him – "My God, my God, why have you forsaken me?" – we gain a touch point of the ugliness of sin.

As Jesus cried out the words of Psalm 22:1 on the cross, he was expressing trust in God (v. 8), knowing he has agreed to be abandoned to the depth of sin's consequences in order to redeem us from the reversal.

When he cried out these words, the biblically literate bystanders would have known he was proclaiming that he was the Messiah, that he was entering into David's poignant terror of abandonment as a messianic destiny. However, given the darkness of the hour, they would not have fully understood it all at that time.

Like the scapegoat in Leviticus 16, and as Isaiah 53 details in messianic application, all of the world's sin was being laid on his body. Since sin is the absence of God's full presence, the Father, in his goodness, had to turn his back on the Son at this point, for he cannot look on sin. As well, the Holy Spirit, being holy, had to abandon Jesus at this moment, in order for the Son to fully identify with the abandonment of sin. To be "holy" is to be "set apart" into God's presence, and here Jesus was embracing the antithesis – taking onto his person all human profanity.

In Isaiah 59:1-2, we read the following:

Surely the arm of the LORD is not too short to save,

nor his ear too dull to hear.

But your iniquities have separated

you from your God;

your sins have hidden his face from you,

so that he will not hear.

Sin, being the absence of God's full presence, being the realm of self-chosen separation, is where all communication with God is cut off. It is the realm of total abandonment, of total darkness, where the power to live in the light is cut off. In referring to Christ in 2 Corinthians 5:21, Paul tells us that "God made him who had no sin to be sin for us, so that in him we might become the righteousness of God." In fulfilling the Levitical requirements for a sin offering, as John the Baptist prophesied (see John 1:29), and as Hebrews 9:11-28 further details, Jesus became the spotless Lamb of God to pay sin's penalty once and for all.

Jesus paid the price of redemption, which meant the ability to buy us back out of slavery, and that price meant death. It meant the satisfaction of God's justice to let *moth tamuth* finish its course and thus kill sin by killing death. And the only way to satisfy the ethics of choice of *moth tamuth* was for God himself to take on the likeness of a man, die for the cost of sin, and rise again from the dead, thus conquering it after its sting has been removed. Indeed, in John 19:28-30, just before Jesus breathes his last, "knowing that all was now completed," he says, "It is finished." The Greek tense here is *tetelestai*, or the perfect indicative passive of the verb *teleo*. It signifies a work fully completed, or as some translate it, "paid in full." Jesus was fully in control, choosing to die, once our debt of sin has been fully paid through his suffering. He chose to enter the realm of abandonment on our behalf.

Thus, we have here the most remarkable point of all Christian theology in my mind. As sin breaks relationships, God chose to break the relationships within himself as Trinity for a brief season, in the face of the devil's greatest pretense of strength. We as human beings do not have the power to heal brokenness, but God does.

The Power of Unbroken Trust

When Jesus gave up his last breath, the curtain in the temple was torn in two and the earth shook (see Matthew 27:50-51). As Hebrews 10:19ff tells us, it signaled the breaking down of the barrier between man and God. Jesus' death opened the way for us to have direct access to God the Father.

Colossians 2:6-15 addresses this power conflict:

> So then, just as you received Christ Jesus as Lord, continue to live
> in him, rooted and built up in him, strengthened in the faith as you
> were taught, and overflowing with thankfulness.

See to it that no one takes you captive through hollow and deceptive philosophy, which depends on human tradition and the basic principles of this world rather than on Christ.

For in Christ all the fullness of the Deity lives in bodily form, and you have been given fullness in Christ, who is the head over every power and authority. In him you were also circumcised, in the putting off of the sinful nature, not with a circumcision done by the hands of men but with the circumcision done by Christ, having been buried with him in baptism and raised with him through your faith in the power of God, who raised him from the dead.

When you were dead in your sins and in the circumcision of your sinful nature, God made you alive with Christ. He forgave us all our sins, having canceled the written code with its regulations, that was against us and that stood opposed to us; he took it away, nailing it to the cross. And having disarmed the powers and authorities, he made a public spectacle of them, triumphing over them by the cross.

After the tree of life is restored in the last chapter of Revelation, the apostle John says, "No longer will there be any curse" (22:3). Thus we return to the promise of Genesis 3:15 – that the seed of the woman will crush the head of the serpent, but only after being smitten first. Jesus was smitten to pay the price of the curse in full, nailing its debt to the cross as a public notice to the ancient serpent that his power has been disarmed. The Son of Man met the requirements of the Law in full, and in his resurrection he sets the captives free.

To know this power is to know the power of unbroken trust.

It is the only power that can secure the final and complete forgiveness of sins. It is to know the power of biblical ethics rooted in creation and restored to us in redemption.

When Jesus became sin for us on the cross, and gave up all power of deity, how was it possible for him to withstand the fury of the ancient serpent? How possibly could he have taken onto himself all of human sin – with its blood, betrayals, abandonments and curses – onto his tortured body, into his soul, cast away from the presence of God the Father and without recourse to the power of the Holy Spirit? How could he maintain his integrity when his eternal relationship with God the Father was broken at this, the most crucial, moment? To grasp what Jesus did here is to understand why and how the eternal God can relate to us in our humanity and brokenness, and how he is sovereign at the same time.

The power at play is the ethics of unbroken trust. Because of the eternal and unsullied relationships within the triune nature of God the Father, Son and Holy Spirit, and because of the fullness of communication rooted in the power to give and the power to live in the light, trust was phenomenally in place. Jesus, Son of Man and Son of God, though abandoned on the cross, had so fully chosen in his humanity the obedience to the Father, the good God of creation, that he could not act otherwise. His trust in the Father was unbroken even as his body was about to be broken. This to me is the greatest mystery of all – God becoming man on our behalf.

Trust in the triumph of goodness, rooted in the history of relationship with the good God, trumps the power to take and destroy.

Unbroken trust cannot be broken by the ancient serpent.

The devil's highest pretense of manipulative power could not reach up to touch the deepest point of God's weakness – the devil could not touch the power of the reversal of the reversal. Here the power of biblical ethics – of the power to give and its cognates – is seen as the deepest power in the universe, that which underscores true spiritual warfare against the ancient enemy.

And this mystery, rooted in the power to give and the power to live in the light, is what secures the power of informed choice. This gift of human freedom is where, due to the trustworthiness of God, we fully choose to believe, and we come to a chosen point where we cannot choose otherwise. When we come to such a point, especially as we love hard questions starting with ourselves, we cannot hate our enemies; we can only embrace the power to love them as Christ has loved us. We become willing to imitate Christ's love as he laid his life down for his enemies. We cannot embrace bitterness, but rather we flee it and forgive others as God in Christ Jesus has forgiven us.

If but a whisper of this theology were to infect a small number of Christians who wish to be salt and light in the culture, we could turn the nation right side up for the Gospel of Jesus Christ, and even the pagans would thank us.

The Power to Forgive Versus the Impotence of Distrust

After I addressed the Mars Hill Forum in 1995 with Kate Michelman, President of NARAL, I wrote her briefly. She had stated how her husband's abandonment forced to abort their fourth child. I gently suggested that if we do not forgive those who have betrayed us, we will forever be embittered, and thus, slaves to their sins. Our unforgiveness allows them still to control us. In order to be free, we need to exercise the power to forgive, as Jesus forgave his enemies and all humanity on the cross, as Stephen forgave his killers even as they stoned him to death (see Acts 7:60).

To import trust into an untrusting world is the essence of the good news, and it is radical. The cross is the fulfillment of the conflict prophesied in Genesis 3:15, where radically different definitions of power are at stake – the power to give versus the power to take. And the power to give is the

228

predicate for the power to forgive, which is what the cross does on our behalf. Do we trust in unbroken trust, in the power to give and forgive, or do we trust in the power to take before being taken?

The power to forgive is a choice, and we are empowered to make that choice through Jesus.

◆ ◆ ◆

Epilogue
The Six Pillars of Honest Politics

The Six Pillars of Biblical Power: Real Theology for the Grass Roots can transform lives and nations in their simplicity and biblical depth. In this book I have sought to give a brief profile of such theology. It sets the stage for another book, *The Six Pillars of Honest Politics: And the Power of the Pre-Partisan*. Then, in a companion work, *Jesus, in the Face of His Enemies: A Paradigm Shift for Overturning Politics as Usual*, the six pillars percolate everywhere, even if not explicitly identified as such.

For those of us who are biblically rooted Christians, as we live these pillars, we need to be salt and light in the political world, serving as an invitation to the true politics of the kingdom of God – seeking to advance the religious, political and economic liberty for all people equally.

One starting point would be to have churches and Christian leaders join in an Affirmation of the Six Pillars of Biblical Power:

1. *The power to give*: We believe that the Creator, *Yahweh Elohim*, the Lord God Almighty, our heavenly Father, employs his unlimited power to give to and equally bless all people as image bearers of God. The power to give is modeled in the faithful marriage of one man and one woman, in parenthood, and is the basis for trust in human society.

2. *The power to live in the light*: We believe that the Lord God said, "Let there be light," and there was light. As darkness and the prince of darkness flee the light, we embrace the power to live in the light of God's presence, open and accountable to all people in all we believe, say and do.

230

3. *The power of informed choice*: We believe that the Lord God gives us all the power of informed choice, to say yes to the good of freedom and life, and no to the evil of slavery and death.

4. *The power to love hard questions*: We believe that the Lord God gives us the freedom and power to pose hard questions of him, and of one another, in Christian community. This is the power of sanctifying integrity.

5. *The power to love enemies*: We believe that the Lord Jesus loved the world when we were yet enemies of the truth, drowning in a sea of broken trust. Now, as believers, we are empowered by the Holy Spirit to love those who are, at present, enemies of the Gospel.

6. *The power to forgive*: We believe that the power to give is restored to the broken world through the power to forgive, purchased in the life, death and resurrection of the Lord Jesus. Thus, we as believers are called to extend this forgiveness to the broken world, by the power of the Holy Spirit, and in celebration of the mercy that triumphs over judgment in the second coming of Jesus.

Then, the next step would be to see how many leaders in politics would join in an Affirmation of the Six Pillars of Honest Politics:

1. *The power to give* affirms that the unalienable rights of life, liberty and property are given by the Creator to all people equally, and leaders in human government should serve such a gift.

2. *The power to live in the light* means leaders in human government at every level should be as fully transparent as possible.

3. *The power of informed choice* is rooted in an honest definition of terms in political debate, providing a level playing field for all ideas to be heard equally, apart from which political freedom is not possible.

4. *The power to love hard questions* is in place when political leaders honor and answer those who pose them the toughest questions.

5. *The power to love enemies* recognizes that even the harshest of political opponents share a common humanity and are to be treated with respect.

6. *The power to forgive* recognizes the need to address our individual and societal transgressions against one another, and to work toward justice and reconciliation.

These six pillars are by definition pre-partisan. In other words, they set the foundation for healthy partisan debates over public policy, in service to the consent of the governed. The deepest partisanship is the creation of a level playing field for all partisan ideas to be heard equally, where the pursuit of truth in any and all matters becomes possible.

Political candidates who live and articulate the substance of these pillars, regardless of political party, and in contrast with those who do not, deserve to be elected.

When these six pillars are examined, is there anything in them that is not attractive to all people of good will? This is equally true for the atheist who may not like the mention of the Creator, yet likewise seeks to have his or her unalienable rights of life, liberty, property and the pursuit of happiness protected. What other source is there for these rights? Out of unalienable rights comes the freedom for the atheist and all others to be who they are as political equals, under the rule of law in the United States.

The question concerning the nature and role of the Creator became central in a February 1997 Mars Hill Forum at my alma mater, Gordon-Conwell Theological Seminary. My guest was Nadine Strossen, then President of the American Civil Liberties Union (ACLU). Nadine quoted the language of the Declaration of Independence that names the Creator as the Source for unalienable rights. This citation and definition of these rights are what makes the United States unique, even to this day. Nadine and I agree that such rights transcend human government, but she does not profess belief in the God of the Bible as I do. And the text of Genesis 1-2, which names the Creator, proves to be the original historical text that assumes unalienable rights. Despite our different perspectives, we agree on the universal nature of these rights and how every person is due them equally.

The question was also central in an April, 2007 Mars Hill Forum on church and state at Patrick Henry College in Virginia. My guest was Barry Lynn, executive director of Americans United for Separation of Church and State. I set a proper historical backdrop to the Jeffersonian language of the "wall of separation between church and state," noted its improper use since the 1947 *Brown* v. *Board of Education* U.S. Supreme Court decision, but especially that it is a negative metaphor, rooted in a negative freedom.

So I suggested we need a new and positive metaphor for church and state – "a level playing field for all religious and political ideas to be heard equally" – an idea rooted in the third pillar of biblical power, the third pillar of honest politics. Whereas Barry was not ready to change the name of his organization accordingly, he heartedly embraced such a level playing field in so many ways in our discussion. He was deeply appreciative of an opportunity, on equal footing and graciously, to discuss this issue. A level playing field provided for in the ethos of the Mars Hill Forum series.

In *The Six Pillars of Honest Politics*, I conclude its trajectory with a proposal to reduce state and federal law by over 99 percent, where I have actually done so. I took the Connecticut Constitution, and General Laws of 2006, some 17,000 pages with footnotes, and cut it to just over 33 pages. I also took the United States Constitution, and the General Statutes, as of 2006, some 48,000 pages, and cut it to under 25 pages. The fruit of this leads to simplicity and justice in the law; to the constitutional protection of marriage, the unborn and the family; for vital economic liberty and prosperity and thus the power to truly serve the poor and needy; and for a secure national defense where we defend our local liberties and affirm liberty where sought internationally. And the political strategy on how to accomplish this is best modeled in *Jesus, in the Face of His Enemies*.

All with the prior foundation of the six pillars of biblical power in place. In the name of Jesus.

◆ ◆ ◆

Made in the USA
Charleston, SC
23 October 2012